INVISIBLE
WOMEN

INVISIBLE WOMEN

Junior Enlisted Army Wives

MARGARET C. HARRELL

RAND

Library of Congress Cataloging-in-Publication Data

Harrell, Margaret C.
    Invisible women : junior enlisted Army wives / Margaret C. Harrell.
      p. cm.
    "MR-1223"
    Includes bibliographical references.
    ISBN 0-8330-2880-4
    1. Army spouses—United States—Interviews. 2. United States. Army—Military
life. I. Title: Junior enlisted Army wives. II. Title.

U766 .H32 2000
355.1'086'550973—dc21

00-055264

RAND is a nonprofit institution that helps improve policy and decision-making through research and analysis. RAND® is a registered trademark. RAND's publications do not necessarily reflect the opinions or policies of its research sponsors.

Cover design by Eileen Delson La Russo

Published 2000 by RAND
1700 Main Street, P.O. Box 2138, Santa Monica, CA 90407-2138
1200 South Hayes Street, Arlington, VA 22202-5050
RAND URL: http://www.rand.org/
To order RAND documents or to obtain additional information, contact
Distribution Services: Telephone: (310) 451-7002;
Fax: (310) 451-6915; Internet: order@rand.org

Contents

Tables

Preface

In the best of circumstances, military manpower policy is crafted by policymakers with input from military personnel managers, analysts, and military leadership with an in-depth understanding of the life experiences and views of junior enlisted personnel. It is plausible to expect that some policymakers attribute the attitudes and experiences of these young soldiers to particular features, such as youth or lack of advanced education, and thus believe themselves able to empathize with this population group by recalling their own parallel life experiences. However, this approach oversimplifies the life experiences of these families and neglects the reality that most policymakers and professional managers have never experienced the compendium of problems these couples face, such as youth, lack of education, financial difficulties, emotional and physical distance from extended family, and invisibility in a large bureaucracy.

At the center of this book are the personal stories of three junior enlisted spouses, told in their own voices and selected to emphasize the dilemmas numerous enlisted families face. The stories provide insight into the experiences and attitudes of some junior enlisted families. Those who live a military lifestyle—at any pay grade—will find these stories both useful and engaging. Some junior enlisted personnel and their spouses will recognize themselves in these stories, and others in the military community will gain a better understanding of problems they may have seen. Additionally, these insights help provide some human context for official statistics and should be of interest to the military leadership; personnel managers; analysts; and policymakers involved in the recruiting, retention, and management of junior enlisted personnel and their families, as well as to Congress and the media.

These stories were excerpted from a long series of interviews conducted during research for a dissertation that addressed the roles and experiences of Army spouses. This research included 105 recorded and transcribed interviews with military spouses, as well as less formal interviews and discussions with military personnel, spouses, and other individuals in the military community. The author also spoke with numerous other spouses and soldiers during Enlisted Spouses Club meetings, Officers' Spouses Club meetings, visits to Army Community Services facilities, and various other gatherings. This research also included an extensive review of the archives of local military and civilian newspapers.

The dissertation research was supported in part by the University of Virginia's Center for Children, Families, and the Law; the National Science Foundation; RAND; and the Forces and Resources Policy Center of RAND's National Defense Research Institute, a federally funded research and development center sponsored by the Office of the Secretary of Defense, the Joint Staff, the Unified Commands, and the defense agencies. While the research was not part of a RAND project and was not funded through the Department of Defense, the Army officially acknowledged it and enabled it to occur. At each of the research locations, the author was formally acknowledged by the local military leadership and was approved for interviews and discussions with military personnel, civilian Department of Defense employees, and military dependents. While the research was not part of a RAND project and was not funded through the Department of Defense, the Army facilitated the interviews and discussions with military personnel, civilian Department of Defense employees, and military dependents.

Acknowledgments

I found the local support and endorsement of commanders at Ft. Stewart, Georgia, and at Ft. Drum, New York, as well as the assistance of personnel from Army Community Services and others at these installations invaluable to this research.

Like many ethnographic works, this product resulted from candid conversations with the women featured in this work, as well as with many other Army spouses, Army officers, and professionals who work in the Army and local civilian communities. Although confidentiality precludes the mention of these individuals by name, I deeply appreciate the time they spent with me and the positive attitude they showed toward this research. Most of the interviews with Army spouses were conducted in their homes, and many of these spouses both welcomed and befriended me.

This work benefited from the involvement of my academic committee members from the University of Virginia, professors Susan McKinnon (Anthropology), Peter Metcalf (Anthropology), Charles Perdue (Anthropology), and Sharon Hays (Sociology), as well as from the extremely constructive review by Professor Laura Miller (Sociology), University of California at Los Angeles.

The support and encouragement of RAND colleagues Susan Hosek, former Program Director, Forces and Resources Policy Center, and her successor, Susan Everingham, were also very important to this work. Jerry Sollinger contributed the title and helped to develop this piece from a chapter of an academic dissertation. Jennifer Sloan provided helpful comments in the initial compilation of the transcribed material, and Shirley Lithgow painstakingly transcribed the interviews conducted. The cover is the work of Eileen LaRusso and John Warren, and the entire document benefited from the administrative assistance of Hjordis Blanchard. Finally, Phyllis Gilmore edited the book and prepared it for publication.

Additionally, Pamela Stevens transcribed many of the spouse interviews and Margaret L. M. Cecchine reviewed an early version of the transcribed material.

The field research for this work was made possible, in part, by a dissertation seed grant from the Center for Children, Families, and the Law, University of Virginia, and a dissertation research grant from the National Science Foundation.

Finally, my love and thanks to Mike and Clay, who encouraged this work and tolerated my absence from home for so many weeks, and to Tommie, whose arrival was effective motivation.

Chapter 1
Introduction

This book differs markedly from what many think of as a typical RAND report—a heavily quantitative analysis of a public policy issue. Rather, this document tells a story—three stories, actually—of what it is like to be the wife of a junior enlisted soldier in today's U.S. Army. Most unusually for RAND, the book tells this story largely by using the words of three young women who are married to junior enlisted soldiers.

This story is important for those charged with crafting personnel policy for the military services to hear. Taken together, these narratives open a window into the lives of young enlisted families that policymakers rarely, if ever, have an opportunity to peer through. Although told by individuals and highly personal, these stories extend beyond the three women who tell them. The problems they face, their perceptions (and misperceptions) of the Army, and the concerns they have both make for compelling reading and bring an indispensable human dimension to the need for, and effects of, policy on a very important segment of the group that the policies are intended to serve.

BACKGROUND OF THE RESEARCH

These stories are excerpted from a dissertation regarding the expectations for and roles of U.S. Army spouses. That research involved taped and transcribed interviews with over one hundred Army spouses, as well as extensive discussions and time spent with Army personnel and civilians who work in the Army community.

Why the Army?

To reduce this research to a size and scope consistent with the time and resources available, it was necessary to select a single service for research. This work concentrates upon Army spouses. Any of the services could have served as a source of spouses; however, the Army was chosen for a number of reasons. The Air Force has the lowest percentage of enlisted service members because its primary need is for pilots and because of the associated educational requirements. The Marine Corps held a certain appeal, because it is most focused on the enlisted level and because, in the 1990s, Marine Corps leadership considered precluding the recruitment of married men as enlisted Marines. However, the Marines are the smallest branch of the armed forces and have few stateside posts. The Army and the Navy are both advantageous choices because they contain a large number and high percentage of enlisted personnel, as well as a diversity of research locations from which to select. Given the opportunity to focus on only one service, the Army was chosen because a better quality of product could be produced in a timely manner. The author is a daughter of an Army officer and therefore has a background in Army culture and language. This knowledge allowed the author to understand more of the context of the issues and prevented any delay necessary to learn service-specific organizational structure, traditions, and terminology. Also, prior research conducted with the cooperation of the Army resulted in its willingness to provide entrance into the Army community, an endeavor that can be quite time consuming and not always successful for scholars wishing to study military personnel.

A Word About Locations

Initial investigation suggested that the selection of research locations was critical to the research effort. It was important to split the research between two locations, both to ensure that data were not limited by area-specific issues and to guarantee confidentiality. Past research experience also indicated that individuals were more comfortable and more candid talking to researchers if they knew that the research included multiple locations.

The following criteria determined the locations. First, it was important that the location include operational units, as opposed to training units. Operational units are structured by rank, from the most junior enlisted personnel to the commanding general. The author's prior research and personal experience suggested that the role of spouses rested on both the rank and the job of the uniformed military member. In contrast, training organizations comprise the "cadre" and the students. The students consist of, and act as, groups of peers and often have considerably less vested in the community, given that they may remain at that post for as little as a few weeks or as much as only ten or eleven months. Second, given the choice of an operational unit, it was important to find a location where the operational unit was deploying with relative frequency, because frequent deployments increase both the role of military spouses and the stresses that they encounter. Third, an Army post removed from any major metropolitan areas was desirable, the hypothesis being that greater distance from a major metropolitan area would increase both the spouses' dependence on and involvement in the military community. Fourth, it was useful to avoid locations perceived to be "over-studied" because of concern about potential interview subjects who were tired of researchers. This concern eliminated, for example, Ft. Bragg, North Carolina.

Most of these criteria were designed to select a location with military families living in potentially stressful situations. This was done for several reasons. First, almost all military families spend some time at such locations. Thus, to select a location where families did not experience these pressures was to ignore the more difficult periods that military families endure and thus to paint a misleadingly rosy picture. Second, by selecting such research sites, this research could determine the extent to which the military community and its resources can address and ameliorate the problems that military families face.

These criteria resulted in the selection of two bases typical of bases with deployable units. While the results cannot be generalized across the entire Department of Defense or even the entire Army, these stories do provide insights into the lives of junior enlisted spouses, given that the majority of junior enlisted soldiers are assigned to bases like these.

SELECTION AND DESCRIPTION OF RESEARCH LOCATIONS

Application of the criteria set to the Army installations led to the selection of Ft. Stewart, Georgia, and Ft. Drum, New York. The following text describes the characteristics of these locations. It is important to remember that military personnel rotate through different locations and, thus, that the military personnel and families at these locations are not themselves specific to that geographical region. The result is a diverse mixture of uniformed personnel and families at all military bases.

Ft. Stewart, Georgia

Ft. Stewart is home to the frequently deployed 3rd Infantry Division and is located approximately 40 miles from Savannah, Georgia. Although Ft. Stewart, which covers 279,270 acres, is the largest Army installation east of the Mississippi, much of the area is swampland. Approximately 15,900 soldiers are stationed at Ft. Stewart, and there are 3,356 civilian employees on post.[1]

Ft. Stewart has been in existence (although formerly called Camp Stewart) on an on-again, off-again basis since 1940.[2] As the Vietnam conflict came to a close in the early 1970s, Ft. Stewart was largely inactive, having been used mostly as a training camp for the prior decades. However, in 1974, the 1st Battalion of the 75th Infantry Regiment (Ranger) and the 1st Brigade of the 24th Infantry Division were reactivated at Ft. Stewart. The reactivation of these two historic units carried Ft. Stewart into a new phase. Many facilities were updated, and many of the older World War II–vintage wooden buildings were replaced, although some of these older buildings still dictate the landscape of Ft. Stewart, giving the post a stereotypical mil-

---

[1] Marcoa Publishing, Inc., Ft. Stewart and Hunter Army Airfield, 1996.

[2] The Ft. Stewart background material is excerpted largely from material that the Ft. Stewart Public Affairs Office provided, as well as from the official Ft. Stewart Web site (http://www.stewart.army.mil).

itary appearance. In 1980, the 24th Infantry Division was designated a mechanized division and became the heavy infantry division of the then–new Rapid Deployment Force (RDF). The RDF role dictates the atmosphere at Ft. Stewart, given that the mission of the RDF is to be prepared to deploy to anywhere on the globe at a moment's notice. The commanding general of the division has described its role as the "head of the spear" of rapid deployment.

In 1996, the 3rd Infantry Division replaced the 24th Infantry Division at Ft. Stewart and continued the role as the heavy infantry division of the RDF, but for most individuals stationed at Ft. Stewart, this amounted to little more than a name change. The mission remained the same; individuals were not reassigned or moved to different units; and some battalions did not even change their designations. The tone of Ft. Stewart, where any international crisis reported on the evening news may mean that the unit is about to deploy, is the same. Indeed, deployment is a constant fact of life for those at Ft. Stewart. During Operation Desert Storm, the entire division deployed to the Persian Gulf, leaving Ft. Stewart and the surrounding areas virtually a ghost town, as many of the younger spouses left the area to stay with relatives during the deployment. Since then, the division has participated in missions in Kuwait, Bosnia, and Egypt, mostly on three- to six-month rotations, and portions of the division are currently deployed.

Liberty County, in which most of Ft. Stewart is located, consists of small communities with a total county population of approximately 62,000. The closest town to Ft. Stewart is Hinesville, Georgia, which sits immediately outside the military gates. Hinesville is a small town of slightly more than 30,000 people, who largely depend upon Ft. Stewart as the major employer of the area. Business and industry are limited in Hinesville, consisting mainly of mini-malls, car dealerships, trailer parks, and fast-food restaurants. Thus, employment opportunities are extremely limited. Many of the military families live in Hinesville and the surrounding area, given the insufficient amount of military housing on base, and all the military children attend the local civilian schools after grade 6.

The residential neighborhoods of Hinesville are a combination of trailer parks and suburban areas. There are not many neighborhoods of large or stately homes; several senior officers' spouses noted their difficulty finding a home off post and generally mentioned that their selections were based on either-or choices. Most of the homes were built approximately 20 years ago, although many of the neighborhoods still lack large trees. Certain neighborhoods are occupied primarily by military personnel, and it appears that soldiers of approximately the same rank often reside in the same neighborhood (junior enlisted with other junior enlisted, junior officers with other junior officers or with senior noncommissioned officers [NCOs], senior officers with other senior officers). It is not clear whether coincidence, cost, or comfort with one's neighbors drives this arrangement.

The local civilian population has mixed sentiments about Ft. Stewart. They depend upon the military for their livelihood, which was made very apparent during Operation Desert Storm, when some local businesses went bankrupt because of the deployment and the lack of military left in the area. However, there is also a certain amount of animosity and resentment toward the military community, albeit not necessarily to any degree greater than that found in similar situations all over the country.

Although Savannah is a one-hour drive from Ft. Stewart, few people venture to Savannah on a regular basis, and it is generally considered too far away to commute for employment opportunities. Likewise, although there are renowned resort communities within reasonable distances—Tybee Island, Georgia (1.5-hour drive), Hilton Head Island, South Carolina (2-hour drive), and Charleston, South Carolina (2.5-hour drive)—few military people indulge in such outings, and people complain that the Ft. Stewart–Hinesville location is isolated and limited. Other complaints frequently include the weather of Ft. Stewart, which is hot and humid during the long summers typical of the southeastern United States.

Ft. Drum, New York

Like Ft. Stewart, Georgia, Ft. Drum hosts frequently deployed units and is located in a geographically remote, economically depressed area. Ft. Drum is the residence of the 10th Mountain Division, another frequently deployed operational unit. The post is located in upstate New York, approximately a two-hour drive north of Syracuse. Ft. Drum is another relatively large installation, covering 107,265 acres and including approximately 10,500 assigned military personnel and 2,500 civilian employees.[3] Its mission includes planning and support for the mobilization and training of almost 80,000 troops annually. Most of Ft. Drum is relatively new, having been built as part of the reactivation of the post in 1985. The facilities at Ft. Drum are considerably more spread out than those on Ft. Stewart and are located on primarily wooded and rolling terrain, with a lot of open space.

Decisions made as part of the reactivation of Ft. Drum, in 1985, had a dramatic effect upon the character of military housing for the post. Ft. Drum has a relatively large number of military housing quarters, but approximately half of the housing is located off Ft. Drum. Although most housing areas outside the post are sited near a local village, there is often little nearby other than a drugstore, a convenience store, and an occasional fast-food establishment. Some of these housing areas are as much as 30 miles from post, which is a considerable distance across roads that are often bad in the winter. These housing areas, which are only for military residents, are managed by civilian contracting companies and are within the jurisdiction of the local police, which has also been a cause of concern. At least one of these housing areas has had problems with violent crime, and they are perceived by the military to be underpatrolled by local law enforcement, who complain of limited resources.

This housing arrangement is unusual for the military. Although there is plenty of room on Ft. Drum to have constructed sufficient housing on the post, this distant and well-dispersed military housing resulted from an effort to win local support for the expansion of Ft. Drum by "spreading the wealth" of both the construction costs and the purchasing dollars of the military residents. However, the contractors who built the housing are rumored not to have hired many craftsmen from the local communities, and there are not many local

---

[3] As of September 1999 (Ft. Drum Public Affairs Office, telephone communication).

businesses at which military families can spend their money. The most unfortunate result of this decision is that a large number of military families are stranded in remote areas distant from post.

Ft. Drum and most of the military housing areas are located within Jefferson County, New York, which is a rural county with a population of approximately 111,000, comprising mostly small towns and villages. More than a fourth of this population resulted from the reactivation of Ft. Drum.[4] The terrain of the area is rolling countryside, punctuated by farms. Although there is a fair amount of wooded area, the effects of the severe ice storm of several years ago are still evident; trees are broken and have been pruned back in often bizarre shapes to remove the dead and broken branches. The result is an almost surreal countryside after the leaves have dropped from the trees.

Like the civilian area outside Ft. Stewart, the area surrounding Ft. Drum is economically sluggish, with few employment opportunities for military spouses. The closest town to Ft. Drum is Watertown, New York, which has a population of approximately 29,400. Watertown has considerably more entertainment options (e.g., restaurants, a shopping mall, movie theaters) than does the Hinesville area outside of Ft. Stewart, Georgia, but nonetheless is still economically depressed and offers few employment opportunities. The jobs that are available typically pay minimum wage and so are considered unworthy of the long drive from the more distant housing areas, even for families that have two vehicles.

The county is a renowned recreational area, with fishing, hunting, and sailing, particularly in the Thousand Islands region, which was known as the "Millionaires' Playground" at the turn of the century. However, the economy of the county has largely depended upon the water, agricultural, and forest resources, and there are few employment opportunities for new arrivals, such as military spouses. Some of the military families do speak positively of the fishing, hunting, and the local resort atmosphere of Sackett's Harbor, a waterfront community, but like the spouses at Ft. Stewart, most bemoan the isolation of the surroundings.

---

[4]Jefferson County Web page (http://www.sunyjefferson.edu/jc/About/home.html).

In fact, with the exception of the characteristics of military housing at the two locations (more is available at Ft. Drum, but most of Ft. Drum's housing is more remote than that at Ft. Stewart), many of the complaints of spouses living in Ft. Stewart and Ft. Drum were similar: the lack of employment or career options, the remote locations, the extreme climates, the frequent field exercises that take their soldiers away for brief separations (two days to one month), and the constant threat of longer (three to six months) deployments. Further, while the units at Ft. Drum and Ft. Stewart deploy more than units at many other bases, some of the characteristics of these two locations also apply to many military bases. The remote location and the depressed economic situation (often a result of the remote location) are generally characteristic of Army bases with deployable units, and it is to these units that the majority of junior enlisted personnel are assigned.

SELECTION OF A UNIT AT THE RESEARCH LOCATIONS

With the assistance of official contacts at each of the research locations, two units were selected for study. At Ft. Stewart, this was an infantry battalion, which consisted of approximately 900 personnel, including all enlisted ranks, and officers to the rank of the battalion commander, a lieutenant colonel. Because this is an infantry battalion, there are no women in the unit. Thus, all the military spouses of this battalion are wives.

At Ft. Drum, to provide some contrast with the all-male infantry battalion, a support battalion was chosen. The battalion selected includes women but deploys with other all-male combat units. At the time of the research, there were 510 individuals in the selected battalion, and less than 20 percent of the personnel were female.

Specific battalions were selected because it was important to speak with spouses whose military sponsors had the same chain of command and deployment experiences.[5] This common experience would enable discernment of individual opinion and interpretation of single events from different experiences and exposures to issues and incidents. However, interviews were not confined to spouses from these battalions. Although enough spouses from the same battalion were interviewed to gain an accurate depiction of life as a spouse in that battalion and to be able to discern the effects of individual personalities from the realities that faced the women married to soldiers in a particular unit, a depiction of life at the overall location was important. Thus, it was necessary to guard against having perceptions marred by the potential selection of a problematic unit. Additionally, obtaining interviews with spouses who had unique characteristics, such as those who were extremely active in the community, and with spouses of higher-ranking officers than were assigned to a battalion required a sample from outside the selected battalions.

Spouse Interviews

The interviews conducted with military spouses are the heart of the broader research effort. The interviews were conducted in a loose, life-history style with very open-ended questions about the spouses' backgrounds and their experiences of, and attitudes toward, military life. An understanding of their prior socioeconomic backgrounds was sought either to challenge or to reassert the perceived differences between the spouses of the officer and enlisted communities, as well as to help explain their differing perceptions of one another. In general, this life-history approach to the interviews provided an opportunity to gain a broader understanding from more-general questions and tended to illuminate the issues that the spouses were most concerned about more than a strict question-and-answer interview format might have done. The less-structured discussion permitted the spouses to indicate the aspects of their lives that they found most rewarding, frustrating, or difficult. This format also contributed to an understanding of the formal and informal networks of spouses, including how, why, and to what degree they interact with one another; how they learned the rules of interaction; and their attitudes toward formal rules of interaction among spouses, including how

---

[5]The *sponsor* is the member of the marriage who wears the military uniform. Hereafter, the *dependent*, or civilian spouse, will be referred to as the *spouse*, and the military member of the family will be referred to as the *sponsor*.

they referred to one another. Hearing how spouses referred to the spouses of higher-ranking military personnel, as well as how they characterized the spouses of lower-ranking personnel, during the interviews provided the basis for a depiction of the cultural construction of gender roles across class in the military hierarchy.

The protocol developed for these interviews was used primarily as a checklist of topics, rather than as a question-and-answer tool. All the interviews were conducted by a single researcher, thus ensuring that questions were asked similarly throughout the interviews. Although the content of the interviews varied somewhat based upon the individual's background, time in the military community, attitudes about their military experience, and personality, most interviews covered the same basic materials and issues.

Selecting and Interviewing Spouses

The sampling of spouses for interviews involved some rather elaborate techniques to ensure that those interviewed would remain anonymous. These procedures were complicated further by Army regulations and policies to ensure privacy. Other limitations included such things as disconnected phones and, at Ft. Drum, the distances between residences and bad winter weather. In all, over 100 spouses were interviewed.

In addition to the standard interviews, three women, whose stories form the core of this document, agreed to participate in more-extensive expanded interviews. These were expanded life-history interviews carried out over several days with the spouse, including accompanying her out of her home and developing a much broader and deeper understanding of her experience in the military community, including a detailed understanding of the financial aspects of their lives.

These particular women were selected because of the relationship between each of their stories, provided during an initial standard interview, and the stereotype regarding the lives of junior enlisted spouses, who are typically considered to be young, immature, lower-class spouses who are in financial difficulty and who have difficulty controlling their reproductive tendencies. In short, junior enlisted spouses are often reputed to be young and immature "big-haired, trailer park babes with too many children" who do not know how to manage their money. This stereotype is widely held by the military community at large, including other junior enlisted personnel and spouses, who often speak disparagingly of their cohorts. Thus, these three particular women's stories were selected for in-depth presentation according to the degree with which their lives match the common stereotype.

The next three chapters provide glimpses into the lives of three women, Dana, Jennifer, and Toni [not their real names]. One is, in many ways, the stereotypical junior enlisted spouse, although her own story does produce some sympathy and understanding for the situation she finds herself in. The second story is that of a very young spouse, who, but for the grace of some solid family financial guidance from in-laws who were familiar with the military lifestyle, could be the stereotypical spouse. Instead, she and her husband are managing, albeit living a very limited lifestyle. The third is anything but the stereotypical spouse. Instead, she is an older, more mature woman with a college degree, past professional experience, and the wherewithal to lead her husband's unit's Family Support Group and to make a difference in the lives of soldiers and spouses within that unit. However, even such a capable, intelligent woman has her own serious troubles, which the military community exacerbates, and she simply cannot manage the household expenses without working in an extremely unappealing job. Hers is a story of personal and professional sacrifice.

These women represent three different battalions. Dana's husband serves in one of the focus battalions. The other two women were recommended by their Family Support Group leader, in the case of Jennifer, and their battalion commander's wife, in the case of Toni.

These women agreed to speak extensively of their experience because of their perceptions that they were generally invisible to the community and because they hoped to affect the lives of other military spouses. With the exception of Toni, they felt that readers were not likely to recognize their stories. Even Toni thought that once she and her husband relocated to another base (likely to occur before this publication might be publicly available), she too would become invisible. Further, all three spouses felt that what they did or said in this interview would not, and could not, affect their husbands.

These stories are the compilation of numerous interviews with the three women. Thus, there are instances in these interviews where they may appear to contradict themselves. To the extent possible, these instances have been noted with italicized comments identifying the material as coming from a later interview or providing information about the changed circumstances (e.g., a recent pregnancy or a job lost or gained). The interviews with these women were taped, transcribed, and then structured from these lengthy transcriptions into orderly representations of their stories. The text of Chapters 2 through 4 comprises their own spoken words. The bracketed text alters their words slightly to provide necessary information to make the statement clearer for the reader. Footnotes provide additional explanations of terms, such as military acronyms, so as not to disrupt the narratives. Very occasionally, a question asked of the women was incorporated into their text, but only when it was consistent with something they would have said themselves or that they mentioned in a different portion of the transcript. Occasional grammatical errors were repaired when the fix was consistent with something they themselves would have caught and repaired had they seen the final product. However, factual errors have been left because they are an important part of how these women perceive the military community. There are noticeable differences in narrative style between the three stories. This variation is attributable to the style and characteristics of the women themselves.

Organization of This Book

The following three chapters are the stories told by each of the three junior enlisted wives. Each chapter begins with an introduction paragraph written by the author of this book to orient the reader to the basic circumstances of the woman speaking. However, the rest of the chapter consists of the woman's own story. Chapter 5 includes overviews of each of the stories and notes the consistencies and differences between the women's experiences. It discusses the degree to which these women reflect the class-based stereotype of junior enlisted spouses that emerged from the dissertation research and the extent to which their problems result from systemic constraints, which should be of obvious interest to policymakers, or from poor personal decisions, which, to the extent that they are characteristic of the youth and inexperience of the typical junior enlisted couple, should at least be understood by personnel managers and policymakers.

Chapter 2
Dana's Story

Dana in many ways is the stereotypical junior enlisted wife. She is recently married, a young wife away from home for the first time, with a toddler and—before the interviews are over—a second child on the way. Like many junior enlisted wives, she lives off post in the only kind of housing they can afford—a trailer. Employment options are sparse, and the need for child care erodes the modest salary she can command in a low-paying job market. She has a limited insight into the intricacies of Army organizations, procedures, and even the bureaucracies established with her in mind. Her physical isolation, limited financial means, and lack of knowledge about the insular culture her husband has joined combine to reinforce her own sense of invisibility.

HER BACKGROUND

I definitely did not come from a military family, so this is a whole new thing for me. I am from Arizona. I miss it so much. I hate it here but I have no choice, and he has no choice.

My dad worked at [the local utility company]. It's power and electricity. [He worked there] from when he was 16 until he retired. Mom worked now and then. Now she works as assistant manager at Wal-Mart. That's how I met my husband, Ted. He worked with her.

My husband is not from a military family either. His dad worked at Shamrock Foods, which is a big dairy distributor down there, and his mom usually stayed at home, but she started working right before he left as a secretary at the church.

[My husband] decided to go into the military to get away. He was tired of it. He had been engaged, and his fiancée dumped him, and so he wanted to get away, and he thought that the Army was the solution, and because he wanted to get away from Arizona. He wanted to see different things. Now, I don't understand why. He had a great job at Wal-Mart, and I had a job at the vet clinic, and I was going to school.

I graduated from high school before I met him, and then I got a semester in business management while we were dating. We started dating the beginning of August. Four months after we were dating, we got married. He was gone for a month for basic training, and he came back for Christmas leave, and we got married on December 27 so I could come with him. We wanted to get married. We were not going to get married until August of the following year, but I didn't want to be without him. [I knew I wanted to marry him.] It just kind of clicked the first time I met him. He said the same thing. It was just there. And I never felt that way before, and he said the same thing, even though he had been engaged before he met me. He said he never felt that way with her. So, I never thought I'd be here, but I am.

I knew he had joined the military when we started dating. He made that decision long before we met, so there was no way he could get out of it. I asked him several times if there was any way he could get out of the Army, and he kept trying, and they told him no. [He's in for] four years. He's got two more years.

RELATIONSHIP WITH FAMILY

[My family] hates it that we have to be so far away. And I hate it that we have to be so far away. Both my parents and Ted's parents live in the same town. And then 70 miles away, his grandparents and his aunts and uncles all live there. It's sad that Eric [our one-year-old son] doesn't get to see them every day. My brother David is 18. He's fixing to move away from home soon. My brother Josh just turned 16. He's still got a couple of years. Ted's brother Chad just turned 18 also. He's fixing to go to college or something, but in the town his parents live, so he'll still be at home. His sister is 15, so she's still got quite a ways to go. So they're all there together, and we are here.

Ted's dad is coming here on the 18th, and Ted hasn't seen his dad in two years. So he's excited. And this is the first chance his dad has had to come see him. He's not going to take leave while his dad is here, but they're going to let him go home early during the days and stuff like that. They're going to the field, but they're not taking him.

My mom is coming in September. She is going to help me celebrate Eric's first birthday on September 15. She came two days after he was born. She came the day I got out of the hospital. Ted hasn't seen her in a year, but Eric and I saw her December 30 through February 15 of this year.

FAMILY PLANS

[Our marriage has] gotten a lot better, but it was really bad for a while. We jumped in head first. We didn't want to have kids for at least two years, and then I got pregnant on our honeymoon. Eric was an accident. That's why we had Eric. That's why I say I wish I hadn't had him, but I'm glad I did, because I love him to death. [But] I really, really wish we could have waited.

It was really bad at first because I guess I didn't really want to take on the responsibility of taking care of a child so young, and I wanted to go to school, and I can't go to school right now. I have to take care of Eric, and then we don't have the finances for me to go to school, so I don't know what to do. I am just 20 years old.

It's hard. This is my first child, and I am already saying it is hard to raise the baby by myself. Just because when [Ted's] not here, it's real tough on me. Sometimes I'm real glad to have [Eric], but sometimes I just wish he wasn't here.

We plan on having two more [kids]. We are going to start having another one when he comes back from Kuwait [in about 9 months], because Eric will be almost two then.

Two months later, on the topic of pregnancy, after she finds out she is pregnant again: This is another one that was not planned.

[I'm not excited] about this baby, because my husband won't be here when the baby comes. He will be in Kuwait, and there is nothing I can do about it. He will be gone regardless. I am due right around the 23rd of April, and he's supposed to be back anywhere from around the 21st to the 5th of May, which it could be anywhere before that or after that, but there is nothing I can do. Unless I am having major complications, they won't keep him behind. [It will be hard, because] this time I am going to need his help. The last time I was pregnant, I didn't have any kids to take care of. Now I have Eric. I don't know how I'll do this. Hopefully, I can get some of my friends to come and stay with me for a little while. [Already it's been hard.] We really were scared that I was going to have a miscarriage for a little while. They told me not to be lifting on [Eric], and I'm like wonderful, how do I do that? I have to lift him. I can't just say I can't lift you Eric, I'm sorry, and he cries his heart out.

If this baby is a girl, that's it. My husband is getting taken care of. He has already said it. He promised me long before we had Eric, a boy and a girl, and that's it, I'm getting done. [If this is a boy], we'll think about it. We are going to think really hard if I want to go through this again.

You can't afford to have them. I mean keeping them is not half as bad as having them. I wasn't too worried with Eric, but now that we are having a second one, I am really worried about whether or not we are going to make it.

FINANCIAL ISSUES

My husband is an E-3. Money is really tight. The military's okay, because they provide everything to you, but they pay you so little, and they expect you to live off of it. When he was an E-2, I tried to get food stamps, and they said he made $100 too much, so I couldn't get them. And I know a sergeant with two kids, who is on food stamps. I figured it would help us out, but they wouldn't even give them to us. And that's weird, because I am on WIC.[1] They go by your base pay, not by your gross net income, which is kind of stupid, because after taxes we have like $200 less.

---

[1]Women, Infants, Children. This Department of Agriculture program provides nutrition and education for pregnant, breastfeeding, and postpartum women; infants; and young children, with participation based on need as determined by income.

[The trouble began when we moved into the townhouse.] We moved into the town house three weeks after we got here, and we moved out in December of 1997. My husband picked it out. He liked it because it was big, but it was $425 a month, which was hard on us because it was more than [our housing allowance], and then the electricity usually ran $100, and we had long distance on our phone, which ran us about $300 a month, with all our family being across the country. And we had our car payment, which was $300 a month, and we couldn't afford it, so that's why they repossessed it, and we had to pay the water bill, and we had a gas bill. It got outrageous. We just couldn't afford it.

We got behind in a payment because the Army took $250 out because he was gone the whole month. So they repossessed the car in March. The Army said it was separate rations. $250. They don't realize that that $250 can cover our groceries for two months. We actually make less money while they are away.

[She provides the LES,[2] as shown in Table 2.1.] This is how much he makes before taxes and before our allotment comes out for rent. They take it out as soon as he gets paid. With the Army, I never know from month to month what he is going to get paid.

Regarding the deductions: The "meals provided" deduction is the separate rats. They're taking it back out. They give it all to you, but then they'll take it back, if he goes to the field. They think that that feeds just him. $200 and some odd dollars can feed both Ted and me and Eric for two months.

Regarding the allotments: That was our rent, the $325. The only way you can stay here if you are in the military is that you do an allotment, and most places are getting like that because they just don't want to handle late payments and things like that.

The $250 is on our repossessed car. We still owe them $9,000. They sold it, and whatever they sold it for, we owe them for whatever is over. [We'll pay that for] years, because we just started paying on it in September.

The $125 is on our tire loan. I get up every morning and take my husband to work so that I can have the car to go to work. One morn-

---

[2]Leave and Earnings Statement (a paystub).

Table 2.1   Dana's Typical Monthly Pay Statement ($)

Pay	Base pay	1,118.00
	BAS [a]	429.00
	BAH[b]	404.00
	Total pay	1,951.00
Deductions	Taxes and medical	171.00
	Meals provided	174.00
	Total deductions	345.00
Allotments	Rent	325.00
	Repossessed car	250.00
	Tire loan	125.00
	CFC[c]	5.00
	Total allotments	705.00
Monthly take-home pay		901.00

NOTE: Here and in the following chapters, this is actually a representation of the soldier's pay, unless stated otherwise.

[a]Basic Allowance for Subsistence (also known as separate rations or separate rats).

[b]Basic Allowance for Housing.

[c]Combined Federal Campaign (a large-scale annual fundraising effort that benefits many of the charitable organizations that serve the military community).

ing I was taking him early, and our headlights don't work so well, so when I came around the corner off of the highway onto the street here, I hit the curb and busted out both of the tires on one side. In order to get them fixed, we got a loan through a loan company and got them fixed. That's the only way we could have done it. We couldn't have done it on his pay or anything like that. It was a $500 loan, and we have to pay $125 for six months, so they are getting 50 percent of their loan. I thought that was really stupid. There is no way I am paying them 50 percent of their loan, but AER[3] wouldn't help us, because they said, it was something about it wasn't bad enough as to where we needed a loan from them, like if the transmission went out or something in the car, then they would give us a loan, but with the tires blown, they wouldn't. I don't think I even went in there. I think I told my husband I didn't want to go in there.

---

[3] Army Emergency Relief. A financial aid program run through the Army Community Services (ACS) that offers grants and loans for financial emergencies but has strict limitations as to what qualifies as an emergency.

He was the one who went in there and took care of it, so I don't even know how it went with them. I just try not to bother with most military things because they look down upon me more than they actually treat me as an equal.

But that's why people give people in the military loans. Because they can do an allotment, and they know they will get paid.

The CFC money actually goes to ACS. We don't have a choice. Everybody pays it. Which is dumb, because we couldn't get a loan through them.[4]

Regarding her income: I have to work. I am a veterinarian technician. I always wanted to be a veterinarian. It takes eight years of school to be one. I can go under the GI bill, but I still need to work. We can't make it without me working. We've had some rough times, but we are doing better now. Financially, it's hard still, but even that is better. We always have unexpected bills, but I have my job now, so it's a lot better.

My salary would depend on how many hours I worked a week, but I made minimum wage ($5.15 an hour). At first, I was getting 40 hours a week. But then they started hiring more people, so I got less, anywhere between $200 and a $100 a week. I paid a dollar an hour for daycare, and it depended on how many hours I worked. A friend of mine watched Eric. But she is pregnant also, so she has stopped baby-sitting, which was fine for me, because I lost my job. But I talked to one of the ladies (her husband is in the same platoon as my husband), and she knew one of the ladies that did baby-sitting, and I talked to this lady, and she said [she'd] take on the same rate that my other baby-sitter was doing, which was a $1.00 an hour, but I never ended up having to use her as a baby-sitter, so if I do go back to work, she said she would baby-sit if she was still there, because the post daycare system has a long waiting list. I went down there to see, and you have to pay a $25 registration fee, and then you have to fill out all this paperwork, saying that your child is up to date on his shots and this and that, and give them beneficiaries, all sorts of things, and as far as I know, they go by your income, and whatever

---

[4]CFC is a voluntary charitable contribution, but soldiers may feel pressured by unit leadership to contribute.

your income is, then they establish how much it is going to cost. It's expensive, and they have two different kinds of daycare. They have the regular daycare, which went from like 5 to 6 and you had to pick them up by 6, no later than that. And I am like, that wouldn't work for me because most of the time I worked past 6:30, and what about when my husband wasn't there, like when he is in the field, like now, he's in the field, and then they had other daycare, which I guess where people would do it in their home, and it was hourly, and it all depended on how much the people wanted to charge you. I said forget this, I'll go find my own baby-sitter.

After she lost her job: They laid me off because I am pregnant. I told her I was pregnant, and slowly but surely she started hiring more people and then told me to go. "We don't need you to work here any more." She didn't say verbally that she was laying me off because I was pregnant, but she said "because of health reasons," so I know it was because I was pregnant. I spoke to some of my husband's sergeants, and they said she can say health reasons, and it will be legal.

OSHA,[5] the health board [says I have to tell my employer I'm pregnant]. See, I had to tell the people I worked with at the vet clinic that I was pregnant, and that was because I was working around animals, but as far as OSHA goes, I was not allowed to work unless I had a doctor's excuse, and I couldn't see the doctor until my pregnancy test from the hospital came back positive. The first time it didn't, and the second time it did, which wasn't until October that it came back positive, and then I didn't even get in to see—you have to go through an OB[6] registration class in order to be seen by the doctor at the hospital, and I didn't go through that class until October 5—and I am not even going to see the doctor until this Friday. So I was laid off way before I could have gotten the doctor's pass to be able to work. They won't see you in the hospital until you are 12 weeks anyway, and I am barely 12 weeks. And then the way they do it you cannot go into labor and delivery until you are 20 weeks along. If anything happens, you have to go to ER,[7] which I was in ER like

---

[5]Occupational Safety and Health Administration.

[6]Obstetrical, obstetrician.

[7]Emergency room.

last week. I waited three hours. I was bleeding and having cramps, and I was there three hours. I thought, "thanks a lot people, I could have lost my baby, and you guys make me wait for three hours."

But [the medical care] is free. I can complain all I want, but it's still free. I would prefer to go to a civilian doctor and to a civilian hospital, but then I would have to pay 20 percent of the cost, which having a baby, it isn't cheap. So 20 percent would probably be like $2,000. And we definitely cannot afford that.

It will be hard now. We sometimes have to call some of our bill collectors and say, hey, look you guys, we can't pay you a whole lot this month, you'll just have to take like ten bucks, and in the State of Georgia, it is legal to do that. As long as you are paying them something, they can't come to see you.

Regarding the monthly bills [See Table 2.2]: It's really hard, really hard. We don't have to worry about our rent because we know that's paid for [in an allotment], but then everything else we have to worry about. I have all the bills in my notebook, and I have a divider for each bill. I have to do this or I get lost. I hated the way my husband had it. My filing cabinet is like this too. I have all the old bills filed away.

Table 2.2 Dana's Monthly Bills ($)

Orthodontist ($1,600 debt)	20.00
Cell phone	45.00
Car insurance	69.00
Power	80.00
Local phone	20.00
Storage unit	40.00
AAFES[a] credit card ($580 debt)	65.00
Credit card (J.C. Penney)	20.00
Credit card (Target)	20.00
Encyclopedia ($1,700)	60.00
Bed	20.00
Car	75.00
Total monthly bills	**534.00**

[a]Army and Air Force Exchange Service (the military store on base; most locations carry the same items as a small department store).

The first is the orthodontist. [When I told my parents I was getting married, my mom] said "if you get married now, I am giving you this bill," and just to get her off my back I said okay, because there was nothing she could do. I was 18 years old. What was she going to do, tell me no? That was how I ended up with that orthodontist bill. As of right now, I think I owe $1,600. I pay like $20 a month. That's all they get. They are not very happy, but they can't do anything about it. Mom always tells me that you don't want to make the same mistakes we did and this and that, but I told her the only way I am ever going to learn is that we do it ourselves. We have already made the mistake of having our car repossessed. Ted and I know that we should not have bought a brand new car. We've known that from the beginning, but we were just too hardheaded to let it go through, but we realize that mistake. We've learned so much from that mistake, and we did file bankruptcy, but it never went through, because we decided we didn't want to. It was hurting us more than it was helping us.

We have the cell phone, which we will be stopping soon, because my husband wants to turn it off. It usually runs about $45 a month. Our car insurance, which just went up to $68 or $69 on the one car we have. We were paying like $50, and now it's $69. And then power usually runs us about $80. We just have local phone, so we just pay about $20 a month. We have a storage unit for which we pay about $40 a month on that. We keep junk in it. Anything that we couldn't fit in here. We used to live in a three bedroom townhouse, which was huge. We are sharing it [the storage unit] with a friend of ours right now. We pay half of it, and we can do our laundry at their house, however much we want. We will get rid of it when we move to quarters, so they have got to get all their stuff out of there. Quarters have a hookup for a washer and a dryer, and we have a washer, but we don't have a dryer.

Then we have our AAFES bill, which is our UCDPP[8] card, and depending on how much my husband spends on clothing and everything, it usually runs about $65 a month that we have to pay on this. The $65 is to pay off current debt. We have about $580.00 on the

---

[8]Uniform Clothing Deferred Payment Plan (a special credit service that can be used to buy merchandise in the Military Clothing Sales Store with no annual fee and no interest rate).

card, and he keeps putting more on it, and I'm going to kill him for it. I am the money manager. I just got upset with him because he went out to that Freedom TV and Stereo place down by Wal-Mart. He went out there and got a loan and bought $2,000 worth of stereo equipment. We can't afford to do that! I got so mad at him. I don't know what to do. I don't know how to tell him we can't afford this. I think he thinks that because he will be making more money [since he's about to be promoted to E-4] that he can spend more money now, but that's not the case. But no, because we ain't got no money.

I have a couple of credit cards myself, but I haven't used them for months. I have just been paying on them since then. I have my Target and J.C. Penney's, and I pay them $20 a month.

We also have this loan to this company for encyclopedias, and I am not even sure how much we still owe. It was $2,000. I think it is like $1,700 now, and we pay them $60 a month. That is if we don't get behind, and we can't pay them. We bought them long before Eric was born. I was about four months pregnant when we decided to get them, because you never know when you're going to need them. And then we thought I was going to go to school, so I thought I would be able to use them a lot.

And we are paying on our bed, which is $79 a month. The people at the furniture store were so nice to us [when we started having financial problems]. They kept saying that they were going to come and repossess it. We called them and said, hey look, we can make small payments every month if you will let us keep it. They said keep the bed and pay on it slowly, but the people we bought the car from came and picked it right up just like that.

And then the only other bill that I can think of is we have a title pawn on our car which we spend $75 a month just so they don't repossess the car, which we owe them $375 every month, but we can't afford to give them the whole amount. So it just keeps adding up. The $75 doesn't reduce the amount we owe them, but if we pay $75 that just holds them off until the next month. It just keeps going like a circle. We have been paying the $75 [for four months], and we can't pay it off. I thought about [getting a loan to pay off the principle], but I just don't want another allotment because we have already got so many allotments, and then the one with the stereo equipment is another allotment. That's another $103 out of his check. I haven't included that because it's next month, and I haven't done next month's bills yet.

We asked [my parents] one time for a loan, for a $300 loan, and my mother went into this long conversation about how she shouldn't help us and this and that. She just went on and on, saying that we're always going to come to them if we need money. So I never even bother with her. I just try to not talk about my finances at all with my parents. But when I call, they go into it. I think they are doing actually well because they had to file bankruptcy some years back when I was younger, and they are just getting out of it now, and she is doing great. I mean she has just bought a new car. She bought one of those 97 or 98 Oldsmobile Intrigues. Paid like $24,000 for it, and then they are looking into buying a house, and they just bought two new horses, and then she talks about how she can't help me pay my orthodontist bill, which was her bill to begin with. She just handed it over to me and told me to pay for it.

They do send things to Eric, though, all the time. My mom just came and visited around Eric's birthday, which was the 15th of last month, and she brought a whole big suitcase full of stuff for Eric, and while she was here, she bought close to $400 worth of stuff for him.

It would be nice if she helped us with groceries instead, but I don't care. They are for Eric. We usually survive on our grocery bill. It's no big deal. We can spend $200 every two months. We have a friend, her husband is an E-5, and she just doesn't understand how we can spend $100 every month and survive, and I said it's easy. If you go to the commissary, and I tell my husband to do this, and he had never done it before, always get the family size things, like the big packages of meat and things like that. It goes a lot further. And then with our bread, we buy like three or four loaves, and we freeze the other ones because all you have to do is pull them out and put them in the refrigerator, and they last forever. And then we get milk and cheese and eggs and all that on WIC, so I don't have to worry about that.

I get four vouchers from WIC per month, and I usually use one a week. They have different things on some of them. I just used one that I got milk, cheese, dried beans. [It tells you what they are good for], and there is only a certain brand, and you have to get certain sizes of things. I get formula from WIC, but they don't give you all that much. All the way up until they are a year, they only give you 31 cans a month. That's like a can a day. My son goes through more than a can a day. He's eating people food now, so that helps out a lot. And I've been trying to get him on real milk. Since he's ten months old, he'll be on it soon with WIC, and so if I don't get him on it, he'll be like "where's the formula?" We tried him on the whole milk, and that just gives him a lot of gas, so we had to go to 2 percent, and he's fine on the 2 percent. And they're probably going to tell me that I can't give him the 2 percent, because they tell you how to feed him, what to feed him, when to feed him, how to break him off the bottle, and this and that. I am like, this is my son, I can do what I want with him.

While I was in the hospital with Eric—for two days, because they make you stay in there two days—I hated it because I wanted to go home; I hated staying there. It felt so cold in there. The nurses didn't care. None of them ever came to see how you were doing. They never came to see if you needed anything. They just expected you to get up and do it all yourself, and then if you had the baby in your room, you cannot take it to the nursery if you have to take a shower. You have to take it in the bathroom with you and take a shower with the baby. And they wouldn't give my husband maternity leave, so he couldn't be there with me the whole time.

Also, you have to go in to WIC. At first, I was going in once a month. When I was pregnant I was going in every month. They would take your blood from your finger and test your sugar and all that. They would take your weight and all that stuff. You have to go to a nutritionist and tell them what you have been eating, and I'm like, does it matter what I've been eating, just be happy that I'm eating, okay. Then when Eric was born, I had to go in once a month when he was real little and had to tell them how much formula he was eating a day and when he started drinking juice, tell them how much juice, what kind of foods he was eating, how many times a day he was eating, and for the longest time they would tell me that he was underweight, and that he was too short for his age. They kept telling me that he needed to get taller, and they had a scale, and they would mark my baby's progress. Eric was always below the average percentile. They'd say, "this is not normal, and I don't know what you are doing wrong." They treat you like you were a child. And now that I am having a second one, now all you have to do is mark off yes I know this, yes I know that, etc., and they will leave me alone.

And it's not just go in and get out. You go in; they take forever to call your name, you have to go in this one room, and they prick your finger and do your weight and all that, and you have to go back out in the waiting room and wait to talk to the nutritionist, and then you have to come back out and wait for them to give you your vouchers, which takes you somewhere around three hours or more.

When I was working, I kept telling them look I have an hour, that's it. And they would say we will try to hurry you as fast as we can. There could be nobody in the waiting room, but I would still have to wait about three hours, and then they got into a new building, and they have a new rule that you can't bring a stroller in there, and only one parent in there at a time. It doesn't matter if you have five kids. You can only have one parent with no strollers. There was one lady that came in one time with a double stroller, and she had a broken leg, and they told her to take the stroller outside. People are idiots.

But as long as I'm on WIC, I always have to go in. And then you have to go in once a year for recertification. You have to tell them how much you are making and a whole bunch of stuff. It's stupid. I do this every year, and we're still the same. A friend of mine is on WIC right now, because [her husband] is an E-4. He is making the maximum pay for an E-4, but I don't know what that is, and he is soon going to get sergeant, but as soon as he gets sergeant, she can't get WIC any more because he'll make too much, even though they are going to have a baby. I don't understand that, because I see some sergeants with one kid that go in there, and they have WIC, and they have been getting it forever. I see some sergeants that have one kid that go and get food stamps, and they have been getting them forever too, which I don't understand.

When I had one baby, the only way I could do it was to get a lot of help from my parents. A lot of help. Like my mom will get some clothes and shoes. And diapers came out of my weekly check. Diapers and baby food and dog food and cat food.

Now I'm not working. Hopefully, [with two kids] we will qualify for food stamps, and I am not sure because I know that when he was an E-2, he is an E-3 now, we didn't qualify for food stamps. He made $100 more than what they wanted. The E-3 pay helps some, but they're taking our housing allowance away because we're moving on base.

[The money will increase some when he gets promoted to E-4], but not a whole lot. I don't even think it will change because our housing allowance is being taken away, and as far as I know it as an E-3, the allowance is about $425. We will be losing money because we pay $325 here, and we pay like $80 for power. [So we have some left over money from the housing allowance each month.] I don't think [the pay difference from E-3 to E-4] is going to be that much. Maybe, maybe, if we are lucky, it will be a $100 more a month.

We just don't go out. We try not to make extra trips. We conserve as much as we can. We barely scrimp by on gas every month as it is. Like before, when I had my job, I would put like $20 aside for gas every week.

Career Ambition and Current Work

I'm not trying to get another job. Not right now. I really don't want one. I like staying home with Eric. My husband is pressuring me to get a job [because of the money], but I know that with me being pregnant and having another one at home that they are not going to hire somebody like that, and you have to tell them you are pregnant, and you have to work there at least six months until you can get maternity leave.

But I look ahead to when I can be a vet. I can't wait. I love working with animals, and I've always wanted to be one. I was practically a straight A student in high school, and I really regret not going to college right after high school. I love Eric to death, but sometimes I just wish I could put him on hold or something so that I could finish some kind of college. Because it would have been wonderful if I had gone at least four years.

I didn't really want to take on the responsibility of taking care of a child so young, and I wanted to go to school, and I can't go to school right now. I have to take care of Eric, and then we don't have the finances for me to go to school, so I don't know what to do. I am just 20 years old. I'll go back eventually. I might be 30 when I go back to school, but I'll go back. See, I have ten years of college for what I want to major in, which is veterinary medicine, so I have a long time. By the time I'm 40, I'll graduate from college.

My husband has talked to the people at the educational center, and they said I could be in school tomorrow, but we can't make it without me working.

HIS FUTURE IN THE MILITARY

He's getting out. He's already told me he's not going to stay in. It's too stressful on him, and on me, and on the baby. It's just too much. But I'm scared to get out of the military, I really am. Because here they provide medical, everything for you. We don't have to pay for medical or anything like that. Like when I had Eric, I paid $32 when I got out of the hospital, and that was it. And the labor and delivery I went through, I probably would have had to pay over $5,000.

He wants to go back to Wal-Mart. When he gets out, we will go back. I want to go back to school, but I doubt that will happen. We've got two more years. I don't know what we are going to do when the two years are over because it's hard, I know the military is hard—he's always gone—but there's always that at least in the Army you have that security; you are always going to get a paycheck no matter what, no matter if he doesn't work a week or something like that, or he's gone. You are always going to get that paycheck, and then there is always the security of not having to worry about medical bills. I don't have to worry about medical bills, which is great. They can provide housing for you, and then you don't have to worry about rent, water, electricity, etc. It offers a lot of great benefits, but there are a lot of downsides to the military, too. I guess that's why people say the military has the highest divorce rate. It's because the spouse, male or female, is always gone. It makes it hard for someone who has children because I am always here to take care of Eric. Eventually, I get tired of taking care of Eric, and I'm like, I want somebody else to take care of him, and [Ted's] not here, so I get mad at him, and there is nothing he can do.

DEPLOYMENT

The longest he has been gone since we've been here was a month, and that was to NTC.[8] He will be gone in January. I'm not real happy about that. If I didn't have Eric, I wouldn't mind. I survived when he was in basic training for four months. If I were alone, I could do it, but with Eric it's harder. When [Ted] leaves, Eric is going to be walking and by the time he comes back he'll be walking and talking, and it will be a whole different story. [Ted] doesn't want to leave.

When [Ted] went to NTC, I didn't stay here. I went home for a month and a half. He was gone for a month. Eric was six months old when I left.

This time [Ted'll] leave sometime between December 1 to the 15th, anytime between there, so it will be real hard. It will be our first Christmas apart, although our first Christmas together wasn't so great either because there was just the three of us, but I will be back home with my family for a little while just because I don't want to spend the holidays by myself. My mom's buying me a ticket. He's taking leave, and he's going home November 14 through the 21st, and his parents are paying for him to go home because he hasn't been home in two years, and he is taking Eric with him, but I won't go home until Christmas.

---

[8]National Training Center (a month-long training exercise held in the California desert).

FAMILY SUPPORT GROUP

I'm a little involved in the Family Support Group. As much as they call me. They don't call me very often. The lady that's the contact—her and I don't speak. We don't get along. And it's a lot harder since I'm one of the youngest wives. I guess they're a lot more discriminating against the younger wives. They don't like to be around you.

Lately, though, one of the girls has been calling me, and telling me everything that is going on, which I didn't really understand half of the stuff that was going on in family support because no one had ever set down and really explained it to me. Like, for instance, I didn't know that they had these things called family team-building classes, which what you do is you go from 9 in the morning until 2 in the afternoon, and your husband gets the day off so he can take care of the kids, but you go in—just the wife goes in—you go in, and it's like a class, and you learn all the abbreviations like MOS,[9] LES, etc., and if you know the stuff, then it is easier for you, and after so many classes they have a test, and if you pass the test, it is college credit, which I didn't know this, and I'm like cool, I can do this. They haven't had any lately, but they are having one on November 3 that I am going to go to.

They asked me to volunteer, when there was that big scare about the war in Kuwait, they got a bunch of wives together to sew the patches on their BDUs.[10] And since I had worked with a seamstress before, they asked me if I would show them how to do it, and since I wasn't doing anything, it was no big deal, but I had to bring Eric along. It was hard, having Eric crying in the background while I was trying to do this. I only agreed to do it because a lot of the guys in his platoon were there. I know a lot of the single soldiers, since he is friends with them. But I don't know many of the married ones. I think it's easier on the single soldiers because they don't have to worry about much of anything, and when they get leave they can just pick up and go home. A lot of them do that.

---

[9]The Military Occupational Specialty (the code for an individual's occupation in the Army).

[10]Battle Dress Uniform (the camouflaged field uniforms).

There are not any women in the Family Support Group that I am friendly with. I really don't know any of them. When my husband deploys, they will have more meetings, but I won't go. I don't feel comfortable around them because they don't really acknowledge that you are there, especially since I am so young. I feel so out of place. A friend of mine, the friend that is 18, she doesn't like to go either because she feels so out of place too because she is so young. And I am sure there are other wives; I am not sure how many are my age, but I am sure there are others who feel just as out of place as I do.

Just like the ball we went to in August. You could tell who was the head of family support and who was the captains' wives and who was the colonels' wives. Because they would just all group together. Like when everybody was dancing, they would all group together and laugh and have drinks and take pictures. You could tell.

But we didn't really get to choose who we get to sit with. Because he was on the color guard, we had to sit with people in the color guard, which I knew maybe one person from there. I wore my senior prom dress, and actually I fit into it better now than I did back then. And I did my hair. It took me 30 minutes to do my hair. I saw it in one of those Frederick's of Hollywood catalogues. It was up in the back and all curly and the tendril in the front.

Rank Among the Spouses

I know one of the captain's wives, and I think he's in the Alpha company, but she's always coming into the clinic with her dog, and she's so nice. She's the only one I know. Most of the officers' wives think they are better than the enlisted wives. I guess because they get more money, and they live in better housing, and they get this and that. They just think they are better, which makes me mad, and then they put you down because you are an enlisted member's wife. I don't associate with them because they seem snotty. There are probably a lot of nice women, but because of the way they present themselves, I don't want to be friends with them.

No, I don't even know half of the enlisted wives in our unit. Like, Ted had a friend, and we've known him since he was a specialist. He got married, and they were going to be Eric's godparents, but then he got promoted, and the way she has treated Eric and the way she's treated Ted, ever since her husband made sergeant, I won't talk to her anymore.

They look down on me, like "she is just an E-3's wife." Like a friend of mine, she is 18, she is married to an E-3. They look down on her a lot because she just barely turned 18, and they have been married almost two years. [They look down on us because we're young, and because] she doesn't have a high school diploma, and she's not going anywhere with her life right now.

I can't get anything done by myself. They wouldn't even let me sign a 30-day [notice] for this place unless I had a power of attorney, which is stupid. Everybody around here is like that. If you don't have a power of attorney, sometimes even if you do, it doesn't matter, they will not even consider talking to you. If you are not the one in the military or if they don't accept power of attorney, you might as well walk out the door, because they aren't even going to look at you.

I just wish I didn't live in a military town because it was not like this at home, and there were two military bases at home, and the town—I mean this town—thrives on the military. If the military wasn't here, this town wouldn't be here. I think it is just the fact that they are so dependent on the military. The military base provides power to most of the city of Hinesville because they own Georgia Power, and I know that during Desert Storm, Hinesville and all the surrounding towns went bankrupt.

ARMY POLICY ON FAMILIES

I don't know what the Army expects of us. They don't tell us anything. They always say that the family is first, but when it comes to family, they just don't care. Like lately with this Kuwait thing, they would call the wives eight hours before the husbands were supposed to be there, so they wouldn't know more than eight hours before that they were going to be on that flight, which was sad. They called them eight hours before they landed at Hunter to tell wives their husband would be on that flight. It would have made a huge difference if they had told us as soon as they knew, like when the unit was getting on the plane over there. I know there were some wives that were gone. And my friend's husband came home Saturday morning at 1:00. She said she waited four hours in the parking lot for him, and her little boy was, gosh, a year old when he left, and now he's almost two years old.

[Army doesn't support junior enlisted families], because for the longest time, we have been waiting for base housing, but he has to get an E-4 before we can get housing.

HOUSING

[After we got into financial trouble because of the townhouse, we moved into this trailer.] I like the trailer park we live in now. [My husband] picked this place. At the time when he showed it to me, I didn't mind, so I said okay. This one I think is one of the much better ones. A friend of ours lives—you go behind the Amoco, there's a street behind it right there, there are a couple of trailer parks—they live in one just down from Amoco, and it's not even nice at all. It's worse than this one right here, and they pay as much as we do.

If they had yards, and they allowed pets, I'd love it. The security level is pretty good too. They give you monthly newsletters that tell you what's going on, and I got one the other day, and it said a couple of the trailers got broken into, I guess because people left them unlocked. I never leave this unlocked. And I'm not real worried because the dog is here with me.

[But] I don't know my neighbors. They're not really neighbor-friendly. The lady across the street that used to live there, she just kind of gave me a dirty look every time I walked out the door, so I thought "forget that." My husband says he has met the people next door, but I haven't because I guess I haven't been here when they were there. They are never home when I am here. Then [there are] the people across the street. They are always having a party. There are always like six cars out in front of their house, so I don't know what the deal is, and they are always home. I guess they never go to work.

I grew up in a trailer, so it's no different. I mean it's different for my husband because he never even lived in one until we moved here, and I'm like, this is no big deal. [He has a harder time with living in a trailer park], and he doesn't like the fact that it is so small. It doesn't bother me at all because it is easy to clean. He thinks it always looks dirty, because he is used to living in a big house. Even when we lived in the townhouse, it was big, it was huge compared to what I was used to, and he said if you messed up something it wouldn't even look like it was dirty.

The furniture is ours. The only thing we bought when we first moved out here was a bed for Ted and me. Everything else we had. The living room furniture cost me $100. We got it from a snowbird (a traveling retired person—we get them from all over the place). They come down during the winter. They were moving, so we got their furniture, and I like it. We got the coffee table for free from a psychiatrist who had it in his office. He was throwing it out, and I said I'll take it.

If he makes E-4, we'll be in base housing, but I am not so sure I want it now. Because we won't be saving but maybe $100 if we're lucky. We don't pay water here. We pay electricity and rent, and that's it. But he has to get an E-4 before we can get [military] housing. And I would feel real uncomfortable for someone to come into my house whenever they wanted to when they wanted to look at it. You have to have your house completely spotless once a month when they come to do a base inspection. They don't consider it's your house. You are living on post. And then your front lawn has to be a certain way. And your house is—there is no carpet. It's all linoleum.

After his promotion: The minute he made E-4, he went in and told them he got a promotion and got on the other housing list. We have been waiting since April of last year for housing. We've been on it since he was an E-1 when we moved here. He got promoted on Thursday [in mid-October] and got his rank pinned on him on Friday, and on Friday is when he went into housing and gave them the orders that said he had been promoted, and they go, okay, here is your housing. This is your number. This is where you are going to be living. We waited over a year and a half to get housing, and the minute he gets E-4, they give it to him, which is just plain stupid.

[We'll be in a] downstairs [unit], because I couldn't climb up and down stairs all day long. I've seen the outside. I haven't seen the inside. They won't let us see it until we go to the inspection. [After the inspection], you can deny it if you don't want it.

We are happy [about the military housing] because it is going to be a bigger place. We are going to have a backyard so Eric can play in it, and I am really happy about that. It will be a lot closer to his work and a lot closer to just everything. We'll be saving on gas a lot. My husband can walk to work in the morning. And I know quite a few people who live on post, which will make it easier. I just wish Ted wasn't going to Kuwait.

FRIENDS

I have two friends. Both are military. One is the one who baby-sits my son, and I met her when Eric was real little. She's my age. And the other one is two years younger than me (18), and her husband is in the same platoon as mine.

HOUSEHOLD RESPONSIBILITIES

If [Ted] gets home before I do, he'll come and get the car from me and go get Eric from the baby-sitter. [Ted'll] come home, pick the house up, and maybe fix dinner. He's not real good as a chef, and sometimes we doesn't even eat because I don't get home until 6:30 or 7:00, and it's so late. But on my days off, I will clean the house and do whatever we need done, and on his days off, he does the same thing. It's only fair, and he doesn't mind either.

HER SUMMARY

Tell me the best thing about being an Army wife. There is nothing best about being an Army wife.

Then tell me the worst stuff. I guess the worst thing is that Ted is not always here. It's hard. This is my first child, and I am already saying it is hard to raise the baby by myself. Just because when he's not here, it's real tough on me.

Chapter 3

Jennifer's Story

Jennifer fits many of the stereotypes of junior enlisted wives. Like Dana, she has not been married for long, has a young child, and is away from home for the first time. Additionally, Jennifer is a teenage mother who left high school to marry and have her child. Her youth increases her isolation from the military community because she is too young to have a driver's license. Nonetheless, she has developed relationships with several other young military wives and is involved with her husband's unit Family Support Group. Despite the fact that her age, limited education, and the expense of daycare all combine to constrict her employment options and thus her contributions to their finances, this young couple manages their money with more aplomb than most. This is in part because of the military experience and guidance of Jennifer's in-laws and in part because she and her husband exhibit a mature financial self-control. Like Dana, however, Jennifer has a very limited perspective into the intricacies of Army organizations and bureaucracies and is physically isolated, financially limited, dependent on other spouses, and largely invisible to the military community.

HER BACKGROUND

The first part of my life I grew up in Freemont, California, and when I was eight, we moved to Auburn, which is close to Reno, and I lived there until I moved here. My mom did daycare in the house, and my dad was a welder. Then they split up, and my mom kept doing daycare, and he kept doing welding. I have an older sister and a younger brother. My sister is a nanny for rich people who live in

California. She goes to college while she's a nanny. My brother is in high school.

My grandpa was [in the military] and so were my two aunts, but I don't know what branch my grandpa went into. I know that one of my aunts was in the Air Force. That's all I know.

My husband's stepdad is a retired naval officer, and his mom is an office manager. I think he just did it [came into the Army] to make something of himself. He has been in since August 12 of 1997—a little over a year. We got married 11 days before he went to boot camp. I was 16. I got married at 16. I didn't think I would get married young. That just happened.

We met when I was in the sixth grade. My husband was friends with my sister. I became friends with him, and we hung around in the summer of my eighth-grade year, and we've been friends ever since, and then we got married. I'm glad I married a best friend and not a stranger.

I had known that he had been talking to a recruiter, and he took a practice ASVAB.[1] We had only been seeing each other for a short time, maybe two weeks. He called me up at a friend's house, and he said, "if I go into the army, would you come with me, and eventually marry me?" So I said, "Sure, why not." We'd only been together like two weeks, and it wasn't a girlfriend-boyfriend thing. I don't know what it was.

He was supposed to leave for Boot Camp on May 31, but he didn't. We got married in August. We told his parents I was pregnant, and we were still going to get married in December, but we talked to his dad, and his dad is a retired Navy officer, and he said do it before because of the medical, and you get more money. So we said okay. By that time, it was only about three weeks until he left, so we had to get it all together and make all those appointments, because with me being under 18, we had to go to a marriage counselor once. California makes you do that. We had to go to the probation department for some reason, I don't know, get our marriage license and all that. There was a big bunch of stuff, and they all required appointments.

---

[1]The Armed Services Vocational Aptitude Battery (the qualification examination required of all potential military recruits).

When I found out I was pregnant, at first I thought "oops." I went in to get on birth control actually. They gave me all the tests. I got a pap, AIDS test, all those tests, and that was the only one of them came back positive. It was good that the other ones didn't come back positive. I was only a couple of weeks [pregnant] because it was the day that I was supposed to start my period.

Jon was at my house because he was waiting for his dad to pick him up. One of the girls I worked with at the Dairy Queen, she happened to be at that clinic at the same time, so she gave me a ride home. I told Jon, and he said, "okay, we'll deal with it," and that it wasn't really a problem.

My mom didn't even know I was going to get birth control. A couple of days before that, she came downstairs after taking a nap and said, "I just had a dream that you told all your friends you were pregnant." I said, "well I'm not." And then the next day I found out. And she even took me back to the clinic the next day. I told her it was to get some test results, but it was really to get prenatal vitamins and stuff, and I had to hide them in my clothes, but I eventually told her.

I finally had to tell my mom in order for her to sign the papers for me to get married, so it was probably a month or so. Not very long before we got married. I said, "I need you to sign the papers for me to get married, and I need it done really soon," and she said, "well, how come?" I said "well, see, I had forgot to take birth control, and I was pregnant." She said, "why did you go out and do something stupid like that for?" I said, "I didn't mean to." I knew that would be her reaction. She would say something like that. Then she ended up signing the papers, and she gave us our rings. This one and Jon's. Because we didn't have rings. They were on her hands, and she said, here. His is just a band, a gold band. I don't know where they came from. This one was given to her a while back, but I don't know where they came from.

Jon's parents got told a couple of days before my mom because I was supposed to tell my mom first, then he would tell his parents, but his mom had caught on, because I had quit smoking, and I didn't want to go anywhere smoky, and I was picky eating. She just caught on somehow. She was observant or something, so Jon's dad asked

Jon, and he said yes. That's how they found out. Then I had to tell my mom because he had already told his parents, so I was kind of pushed into that. Then I finally did. My dad found out the wrong way, I guess, because my sister found out, and she told one of my aunts, and then my aunt called my dad. I tried to get hold of him to tell him I was getting married, but I couldn't, so he didn't find out until after, and he told my sister, "well, maybe when you get married, you'll invite me to your wedding."

Not very many people came. Like nobody really got told. My two uncles happened to come into town the day I was rushing around getting ready for the wedding, so they came. And then all my friends and Jon's best friends and parents were there.

I wore these off-white dressy pants, with a cream-colored shirt underneath that was an interesting fabric, and one of those vest things that was cream and tan, and it tied in the back. I didn't have a dress, and I really didn't care to wear a dress. But if we were to get married again, because we were going to do a big wedding, I would wear a dress. We might do that.

Our families were pretty supportive. I mean, they were not like some parents in stories I've heard about mothers kicking their daughters out and all that stuff. It just all kind of fell together. There weren't any problems. My mom was kind of sad because she was worried that I wouldn't finish high school.

A New Army Wife

And then he went off to boot camp. It was hard being away for that long. I was at my mom's for a little while, and then I moved to Jon's because we took my dresser and stuff and put it in storage, and then I just moved in with them, and I gave my bed to my grandma because my mom bought her a trailer, because she had nowhere to live and stuff. She had gotten herself in a mess. So I just moved in with them, and my father-in-law doesn't work because he is retired. He just does little side jobs at houses, and he could take me to school and to work and stuff. My mom and her fiancé worked, and I wasn't getting along with Mark, the guy she's getting married to. He's okay if I don't live with him, but he's hard to live with. Our personalities clash. So I lived with my in-laws until I left, which was on December 23, right before Christmas.

[Jon] had been here since Thanksgiving. His parents came out in the beginning of December and helped him find [somewhere to live]. They bought this. I hadn't even seen it. I asked his mom if it was nice and if it had all the same colored carpet. She said, "oh yeah, I would put you somewhere nice," so they bought this.

I got here finally on Christmas Eve. Jon already had a Christmas tree and stuff. We didn't have any furniture, but we had a Christmas tree. I was like nine months pregnant, and we didn't have any furniture, and I didn't know that there is a loaning closet [where I could borrow pots, pans, cots, etc.].

Two weeks after I got here, he left for NTC, and we still had no furniture, and I was like nine months pregnant, and I didn't know anybody out here. That was the hardest thing I've done, sit home in this house by myself with nothing in here. It was only a month, and he was on the last flight there and the first flight back, because my due date was close and all that good stuff. But our Realtor, she helped me out. She'd come and visit me and stuff. I didn't have a [driver's] license, so I couldn't go nowhere. That was boring.

He's only gone to the field once since I've been here. He went to NTC, and then to the field, which was about a week long. He's had staff duty when he's gone overnight, but it hasn't been hard. Korea might be hard. That's kind of scary. A whole year. You'd think that you'd get separated—detached—from each other. I don't want that to happen.

I've heard rumors that his unit might deploy, which aren't really ever true in the military. But I have heard one that he might go in May or March of next year, and I've heard another that his battalion is never going. Even if he goes, it won't be bad—only for about three or four months. That's not half as bad as a year, and at least I would know the definite date that he is coming back. Like the first set of people that went over there, they didn't know when they were coming back. It will be a lot easier if you know when they are coming back.

My biggest problem here has been having nobody around. It's really all my problem is here. And me not being able to drive. I wish I could drive, but I can't get my license until I am 18. Because out here, you have to have your permit for a year, and I turn 18 before a year, so it's pointless. I'll just wait. Hopefully, when you turn 18, you don't need a permit.

THEIR RELATIONSHIP

Married life is fun at times, stressful at others. We just go day by day. Depends on things, like if we've missed our family a lot. It's harder because you wish other people were around and all that.

It's tough at times that our family is so far away. There's a lot of stress on us. Like sometimes I don't have anybody to talk to. I don't have my friends that I could just call up. I don't really have a lot of people around here that I could just call up and tell them, "yeah, I'm having a pretty shitty day." It's different. I don't have anybody out here my same age, or going through the same things. Seventeen-year-olds out here are partying, driving around, doing all that stuff.

I basically do everything around the house. He'll get up and help with the baby on the weekends, and he'll clean on the weekends and stuff like that, but I am usually the one in charge of all the other stuff. I just ask him to take care his stuff. I do the rest. It's not much; the condo fee takes care of the yard. They always wake me up with damn mowers, but at least I don't have to wake up and do it.

Most days I just sit around and take care of the baby. Sometimes I go for walks. Today I went for two walks. Then I clean and wait for Jon to get home. Then we go do something. My day is pretty boring. Sometimes Kathy or somebody will come over, and we'll go swimming, or I'll go over to Sandy's house and talk to her or something.

One lady told me that if the Army wanted the soldiers to have wives, they would have issued them in boot camp. I don't care. They don't do anything to me. It doesn't bother me. They just take him away every once in a while. But lately I've been lucky, and they haven't taken him away. But he is on alert, so we can't go very far, and if we do, we have to call them up and tell them, because they could call alert, and blah, blah. He can't drink while he's on alert. It doesn't bother me or him because he doesn't drink very much anyway. He's not 21 yet, so he's not even supposed to be drinking. He does sometimes, but he doesn't do it very often. It's like once in a while, which is good, because I would rather it be that way. Drunks are no fun.

FRIENDSHIPS AND FAMILY SUPPORT GROUP

I have some friends here, like my neighbor one house down, Sandy. And Kathy, she is in our company. I talk to Maria. She is in our company, too. Sometimes I talk to Lori Anne, and sometimes I talk to Tina. Except for Sandy, all my friends are in the company. I met them either from the FSG[2] or just from my husband and their husbands, and we all get together, and then we've become friends.

Sometimes I wish I was back home with friends my age. My friends out here are in their 20s. My youngest friend is 19, which is kind of close. I do wish that I had my friends out here, just for the hell of it, but most of my friends are actually kind of growing up like I am kind of. My two closest friends, they are both named Crystal. One just married into the military, and the other one is going to have a baby pretty soon. They are both older than me though. They are 18.

I've got one friend who just married into the military, and her husband is in Korea. He'll be there for like another seven months, I think. After he had finished training, he came home, got married, and left, and she doesn't really know what married life is really like because he is gone. She has the invisible husband.

I only know two officers' wives, these two ladies that are always at our FSG meetings, three ladies actually. They are married to lieutenants. The others are married to privates or privates first class. They are all lower ranks. I don't know many sergeants' wives. Oh,

---

[2]Family Support Group.

I've met one in an FSG meeting. I mean there are not a lot of wives who come to our meetings. There are like six or seven of them. The others had rather just not come.

I've been told that some officers' wives could be stuck up. I rode with these two German ladies whose husbands are also enlisted, and I was talking to her about how I had lost my wallet, but I found it, and she was saying that she had found a wallet in the Wal-Mart parking lot, and it happened to be a major's wife, and it had like $200 and something dollars in it. She hadn't opened it and looked for the money. She just noticed that it had a military ID and gave it to the MPs.[3] That lady never even called and said thank you or nothing. She said that if it had been a private's wife, she would have probably called. I think that's true too. To a private, $200 is a lot more than to a major, because they got all the money.

All I really do with the Family Support Group is go to potlucks, but I am sure that if I had a problem it would be good to have the FSG around to help me, but I haven't had a problem though. They helped me get to meetings one time when I was here, and they called me. I haven't really needed them yet. It's fun to go to the meetings, though. My husband takes me. Last night I didn't get to go to the FSG meeting. I had to go and finish my GED[4] test.

HER FUTURE

I didn't finish high school, because out here there are not the same programs as there are in California. There is no alternative high school—well there is a high school with a day care center here, but there are something like 50 people on the waiting list, and in the other one I would have to pay for day care, and they don't have independent studying and stuff. So I couldn't do that.

So I decided to do the GED. Actually, with me getting the GED, I will end up in college before I was supposed to graduate, because I am not supposed to graduate until June of this year, but I will probably be in college right around June probably because there is a sum-

---

[3]Military Police.

[4]General Equivalency Diploma.

mer semester, and then there's the fall. I have to wait for the SAT[5] stuff to come back after I take it.

I just finished my GED last night. I think I did pretty good. It was all easy. The only one I am kind of worried about is social studies, because I guessed at the last six questions because I thought the time was up, which it wasn't. The math part, there was only one problem that I didn't understand, and the rest of it was easy. I like math if I get told how to do it. Like if I have been told once, I can do it fine. But if I don't recognize it, I can't do it.

I have applied for college grants. I've put an application in at Georgia Southern University. I'm thinking about putting in an application at Altamonte Technical Institute. They've got a nice campus. I want to work in pediatric nursing or neonatal with the premature newborn babies. I don't want to work with old people, though. I don't want to change their diapers. Babies can't get up and go to the bathroom.

When I left Savannah Tech the other day, I left my wallet on top of the car, and I drove off, and some guy found it. Then the next day, I kept leaving it everywhere. Like yesterday, I left it in the bathroom at the Altamonte Technical Institute, where I was taking my test, and just went back to class. Someone took it to the lost and found. I'm so absent-minded. Like yesterday, I lost $20. I found it, but I lost it. I think it was just all the testing that fried my brain. There were a lot of questions. There were like 64 for each part. And there were five parts. The first day I did writing and an essay. The writing part was multiple choice, and I had to write a 200-word essay. Then social studies. Then last night was understanding literature and art, and science and math. Now, I'm done. I'll get a $500 scholarship as soon as I find out I passed.

Later: I got part of my GED results back. I haven't gotten back the essay and the writing part because it got sent to Atlanta to get graded, but I got a 53 in science, a 50 in math. I know you have to get 40 to pass. No, I got a 59 in science and a 52 in social studies. And a 54 in something. I did fine in all my subjects.

---

[5]Scholastic Aptitude Test.

FINANCIAL ISSUES

If we were still living in California, we wouldn't have half the stuff we do now, if he had a normal job. Because in the town that we were living in, you couldn't get a good enough job and have the benefits and all that. There is no way in hell we would have been able to buy a condo in California, because this one, if it was bought in California, it would be $90,000 to $100,000, and it was only $30,000 here. It's cheaper than renting, that's why we did it. It's good because we would not have had all the stuff that we have, and it would not be as easy as this. We would probably be on welfare or something and living in The Greens, which is the projects. That would not have been any fun.

I do all the bills every month. I learned to take care of the bills and things, I guess, from watching my mom. Balancing the checkbook, I kind of figured out on my own. It wasn't really that difficult.

I can read a little bit of our leave and earnings statement. Most of it I can. Like I can tell how much he made, our deductions, and our allotments, and all that, and how many days he has for leave. I can do that. Some of it I don't understand, but most of it I do. I write all the checks for our bills. So it's okay if he has to go away. It's not like, "oh no, what do I do," not like some wives. Like the wives who don't come to our FSG meetings. They always call for help when their husbands are gone, but they don't ever want to help with anything when they are here. They've never called me, but from the stories I've heard, they call people like our Family Support Group Leader.

I'm not real good at reading all of the LES, but I know what the MGI Bill[6] is. This is money that gets taken out of his check for a year. He pays $100 every month for a year, and he ends up with $15,000 for college for when he gets out. He gets base pay and BAH ($422.28) and BAS (I think that's for food) $230. So the total of what he makes every month is $1,690.91, but then they take out Social Security ($58) and money for medical ($13). Then his life insurance ($16) and then $56 for another life insurance. I'm not sure what the AFRH[7] is. [See Table 3.1.]

---

[6]Montgomery G.I. Bill (tuition assistance).

[7]Armed Forces Retirement Home. This is a charitable contribution.

Table 3.1   Jennifer's Typical Monthly Pay Statement ($)

Pay		
	Base pay	1,038.30
	BAS (separate rations)	230.33
	BAH (housing allowance)	422.28
	Total pay	1,690.91
Deductions	Social security	58.17
	Medicare	13.61
	Life (200K)	16.00
	AFRH	0.50
	MGIB	100.00
	Total deductions	188.28
Allotments	Additional life insurance	56.00
	Total allotments	56.00
Monthly take home pay		1,446.63

Table 3.2   Jennifer's Monthly Bills ($)

Mortgage	334.25
Condo fee	85.00
Local phone	25.00
Power	70.00
Car payment	140.00
Car insurance	105.55
Loan—pay off old house	88.00
Sears credit card	40.00
AAFES credit card	17.00
Food	200.00
Total monthly expenses	1,104.80

The mortgage payment is only $334 [see Table 3.2]. That's not very high. It's less than what you would pay for rent. Everybody around here pays close to $500. We also pay an $85 condo fee. If we have to move, we will rent this out. But if he should have to go to Korea, we will just make double payments, so we can get out quicker, pay this off quicker so we don't have to worry about it so much, but I don't know if he is going to Korea. The payments are so low that if we didn't live here, it wouldn't be too hard on us, if we didn't have a renter.

And we will probably get some money back from our taxes because of our mortgage. There are tax people on post that we went to last year. [One] tried to help us with stuff. She didn't explain stuff real well, but I think if we ask her how we do it, she might tell us. Last year I was the only one that got a return. Jon didn't get one. He almost had to pay. I think I got about $60 back, because I worked at Dairy Queen and K-mart last year. When I was working at the Dairy Queen, I was working at K-mart's at the same time, and going to school. I don't know why I did that.

I've got our phone bill, which is only like $25, because we don't have long distance, because we never put it on, because we know what would happen if we did. We've never had long distance because we figured we would blow it, and we'd be broke all the time, talking on the phone too much. When I get bored some days, I would just love to pick up the phone and call someone. It's nice if I have a phone card, but most of the time I don't. People call me. I can call them collect and they can call me back.

Our electric is probably about $70 in the summertime. We don't have to pay water. And we don't pay garbage. Our car payment is $140. Our car insurance is $105.55. We've got a loan that we took out not too long ago. It's going to be gone after this month. It is just $88. When we went back to California, our house was supposed to close before we left, and it didn't close, so we took out a loan that was in that amount,. And we were just going to pay it off when it closed, but we didn't, and so we just pay it off like this. Oh, and we now have a Sears bill and DPP. We have to pay at least $30 to Sears, and I pay $40. DPP is a deferred payment program through AAFES. We only pay like $17. We only have a $500 limit. We bought our washer and dryer there.

And we usually spend about $100 on food. Oh, it's not a month. It's every two weeks. So it's about $200 a month. The commissary is really cheap. I fix dinner most of the time, except for around payday. We have a tendency to always be out, and we just eat when we are out. It doesn't last very long. We blow our money quick.

The baby's food we get from WIC, but I've never tried for food stamps, because I don't think I need them. WIC is neat. I like WIC. I don't get food any more. I just get baby formula and cereal and stuff for him. It's just neat, saves you a lot of money. About $50 every two weeks on formula. That stuff is expensive. I look at the receipts after every time I go, and I just groan. Glad I'm not paying for this.

EMPLOYMENT

I've looked for a job. It's hard out here, though. It's like everybody wants a job, and there are not very many. I've applied even places that were hiring, and it just seems like that there are so many people looking for jobs, but nobody has like interviewed me yet. I think it's also because I am 17. Some jobs won't accept you unless you are 18. That's a bummer. I'll probably just do college. I might go to the Altamonte Technical Institute and get my LPN[8] thing and just do that, and while I'm working for that, I'll use that money to help me through college. But I've also been told that if you go to the right place, they'll send you back to school to get you to the places that you want to go. Some do, probably not a lot.

In a later interview: I just got a job. McDonald's has been hiring. They keep hiring and hiring and hiring. I really didn't want to work at a fast-food place, but I said oh well, and I went anyway. They take teenagers. And they are giving me 10 days off to go home. They're pretty nice about that. I told them I had my tickets previously, it was all planned before I even went to work there.

My friend Amy is going to baby-sit for me. She charges $1 an hour, but now I just have to find a ride to work. I don't know how I will do that. I know Maria works nights, and she'll take me. I don't know if there is a bus. There is the taxi. From here to Wal-Mart, it costs three bucks, and that's right by McDonald's. That's kind of expensive if you think about how much the gas would cost. I probably could walk if I had to.

---

[8]Licensed practical nurse.

PARENTING

My mom did day care while I was growing up from when I was three to when I was 12, so there were always babies around. And stuff I didn't pick up from that I just kind of learned myself.

I had a WIC appointment yesterday. Well, yesterday was a drive-through one, and that means I just drive through to pick up my vouchers. Sometimes when you go there, they prick [the baby's] finger to check his iron and weigh him and see how tall he is. And they tell me nutritional education. I have been feeding him Cream of Wheat instead of the baby cereal because I ran out of money. It's also got more iron in it.

We'll probably have another baby about three years from now. I don't want to have them real close because of the jealousy thing, and I don't know, it would probably be hard. I want to get one semi-trained before I have another one.

HER SUMMARY

My husband keeps changing his mind about what he wants to do. Sometimes he says he wants to reenlist and do the career thing, and sometimes he wants to get out and get a normal job. He'd probably go to college if he doesn't stay in. I don't know what he is going to do. I guess I'll just have to wait.

[The best thing about the Army] is the benefits and the money, being able to travel for free, that's about all. [I'm not sure what I want him to do.] Military life is kind of fun; I'll get to go see the world—a little of it anyway—but sometimes it's bad. I don't know what it would be like if he had a normal job because we moved straight from our parents' houses to here, and this is all we know, and this is fine with me.

Chapter 4
Toni's Story

Toni is, in many ways, not the stereotypical junior enlisted wife. She is an older woman, in her mid-30s, who has a college degree and professional experience in the workforce. She is considerably more confident and capable than many junior enlisted wives and uses this comfort with authority to act on behalf of others and to lead the unit's Family Support Group. Nonetheless, she still confronts problems very typical to junior enlisted families: She is stymied and frustrated by her experiences in Tricare and by their treatment of her. Additionally, the combination of their financial difficulties and the limited employment opportunities in the area compels her to accept extremely unappealing minimum wage labor incongruent with her professional experience.

HER BACKGROUND

I am from Long Island, New York. I'm a paralegal by trade. I've worked for attorneys in New York and mostly the western part of Long Island for about ten years. I'm not a 21-year-old Army wife, I'm 33. I didn't get married until I was 30, and I knew my husband for five years before we got married. We got married by a Justice of the Peace the month before he went in, and when he came out of basic and AIT,[1] we did it my way, we did it with the dress and the church and the whole nine yards—his wedding and my wedding. We moved down here in May of last year, so it's just about a year and a half I'm here in this little piece of heaven in Georgia [sarcasm].

---

[1] Advanced Individual Training (during which soldiers learn a particular skill after completing basic training).

My husband is four years younger than I am. He turned 29 in July, and I turned 33 in June.

This is my first [marriage], his second. I have an ADHD[2] eight-year-old stepson who was here for five days over labor day weekend. Can you imagine? I managed to get my house clean enough so people could come in without having to climb over things. We haven't unhooked the Nintendo yet. I don't know about it. If I unhook that, then I can't get the VCR to work. I don't know if it goes to the TV. I don't have the wiring diagrams. I have to wait for the husband.

My father worked at Shoreham Nuclear Power Plant. He built the center core reactor, which is a scary thing, because my father was an alcoholic for 21 years, and I used to say I hope they never turn that thing on, because a lot of the steamfitters were either alcoholics or junkies.

I am who I am because of my childhood, and I can get through the Army stuff because I learned the hard way. It wasn't the yellow brick road. My father made a good living. Shoreham put food on our table, so when I was growing up, and they had a nuclear demonstration and everything, and they would ask you to sign petitions, it was a big thing in my family because most of my family were steamfitters. Most of them were working at Shoreham. That put my butt through Catholic school for eight years, my sister and I, paid for our house, put food on the table. Whether it went up or not, it doesn't matter, but it was money in our pockets, and we were okay with it. I have three family members who are still working at Shoreham, now dismantling it, because they decided not to put Shoreham on line. They are ripping it down, but it is still feeding parts of my family in one way or another. My mother is a medical secretary. She went to work when I was in the fifth grade, when I was nine, and I am the oldest of three.

My Uncle Bob was a "Second Louie."[3] He did ROTC[4] in college and he came out a Second Louie. He did two years during Vietnam, but he was stateside. He was Army, but he was stateside, and now

---

[2]Attention Deficit Hyperactivity Disorder.

[3]Second lieutenant.

[4]Reserve Officer Training Corps.

from what I can figure out, because we are not allowed to talk about this you know, he was stationed in Washington, so I figure he was at Ft. Lewis, because that's the only base I know of in Washington. My father, when he became draftable, got married, and then when they were drafting married men, my mother was pregnant with me. Then when it was married, one child, my mother was pregnant again, and when they kept raising the standards my father kept having kids. He was always one kid ahead of the whole draft thing, and it was over by the time my brother was two.

I was raised there, graduated from high school. I got an associate's degree two years ago. It took me ten years to get it. I went right out of high school, and I went to the community college for executive secretarial studies, and I felt like I was in the 13th grade. I wanted to get on with my life. So I went for a year and a half. Said "enough, I've had it, I'm in 13th grade." All they were teaching me was remedial math and all the required courses. "If I do biology one more semester, I am going to go out of my mind." I quit until 1992 [when I] went back, worked my way through it, earned everything I needed and came out as a paralegal on the Dean's List in December of 1994.

I loved being a paralegal, thought it was great. I was making $700 a week tax free because the lawyers are notoriously cheap and won't pay taxes, so I did that for a long time. The last three years I was in New York I worked off the books.

THEIR RELATIONSHIP

I met Vic. He was going through a divorce. It was a hard one. They had no assets to speak of, but the kid they fought over. I tried to stay out of it. I didn't have anything to do with them getting divorced. In the beginning, it was every three or four months she would call up, and she would forget her place—"hello, you're the ex, I'm the current, okay now that we know what roles we play, you want to start over?" Every once in a while, she gets under my skin, and she has to be told who she is again: "You are not Mrs., I am."

WHY HE JOINED THE ARMY

[He almost came into the Army during his first marriage.] She was okay with Vic going into the Army. When they first got married, he wanted to go in, and when he saw the recruiter, when they were married, the recruiter asked him what is your marriage like, and Vic told him straight out, "I am having a little problem." The recruiter said to either work it out or divorce, but don't bring it to the Army. It's not an easy place to be married, in the Army. So if it's not a stable marriage, it is not going to be any better when you first go in.

I didn't know Vic at the time. Three years later, I met him, and he never said anything about the Army during the five years I knew him. During all this time, he was working for a bus company—school bus—drove around three to five-year-olds, back and forth to nursery school and stuff like that. My husband loves kids. He loves them. He thinks they are the greatest things since sliced white bread and Reeboks. They had cassette radios in the school bus, and they all had car seats, and he would put all the kids in the car seats, and he would have Barney tapes and Sesame Street tapes, and as long as they stayed in their seats and they weren't too loud and weren't sticking anything out the window, he'd play the tapes. But the rule was that if you got out of hand, the tape went off. He had the best-run bus in the company, and there had to be about 212 buses. But he had 3 to 5-year-olds that were angels, because they wanted to hear Barney and they wanted to hear stories. And on holidays, he used to get tips from mothers—$40. My mother never tipped a bus driver in my life. She never even thought about it. Vic would come home with $20, $40, $60, $80, and he only had maybe seven kids. But he only got paid for the time that he actually drove the bus. So between 7 and 9, when he was actually picking them up and bringing them to school and then from 2 to 4, he was only getting paid for those four hours, but he was at the bus company for the entire nine hours. $63 a week don't cut it.

And then his ex-wife hit him for $30 a week for child support, which left him $33 before taxes. So one of the schools he drove for was a day camp that ran from 9 until 3, which was perfect, because that was the hours that he was sitting on his butt, so he drove the first shift, worked at the camp, picked up the kids, brought the kids home, came home, had dinner, and would work as a cashier at the local supermarket until 11:00 PM, and he worked those three jobs for about a year and a half.

It didn't bother me so much whether he brought home the money or not. I was bringing home money. We were comfortable. He never said he was miserable. He didn't like working three jobs, but he never said he was miserable, and if we put him through school, and I opened up and kicked money towards him, she'd go after it. So there were certain things that I couldn't give him.

Once Vic was officially divorced, I think that's when he first started thinking about the Army, because my father had said something to him about how he needs to be able to support me. He never directly said anything to Vic because I never told my father we were getting married. We never spoke of marriage to my parents. I won't bring anything to my parents unless I had thoroughly thought it over because I won't stand there with the Spanish Inquisition, 50 questions, and not be prepared with answers because then I look like an idiot. "You didn't think it through. How do you think you are going to get through this if you don't think it all through?" That's how I grew up. It's not, "let's go to Step A and then cross that bridge." It was never cross that bridge. You had to know the absolute end before you even took a step. So that's how I do it.

The day we sat in my backyard and told my parents we were going to get married, my mother looked at me, in my face, in front of him, and said, "I don't think that's the right thing to do." I looked at her, and I tried to remain as cool, I mean poker-faced as I could, even though I was on fire, and I said, "why do you say that?" and I got very Pollyanna-professional. She says, "Toni, I will be honest with you, you are going to work hard the rest of your life. He is not going to be able to keep you in the style that you are accustomed to, you are going to work, and you are going to work hard." This is my mother; we were raised to respect [our] elders, respect your mother, you know. In my house growing up, it was never actually spoken, but you knew if you did something wrong, bad enough, they would kill you and have another who wouldn't do that. It was never actually stated, but it was just understood.

I think what she was trying, now that I look back on it, what she was trying to tell me was that it isn't an easy road. My answer to her was, "Ma you don't understand, he would walk through fire for me. Vic would walk through fire for me." I knew that, and they tell you that somehow you will know when it's love. I knew it, because the man will walk through fire for me. Whatever you want.

So he came home one day, and I'm sitting on the couch. I work nine to five, great job, feet up, Montel, Oprah, or whatever, and he comes in and he throws an Army pamphlet on the coffee table and sits down right across from me and sits there. I looked at it and I said to myself, "Please God, just tell me he picked this up off a brochure stand and kept walking," and all I kept thinking was now he was going to tell me he enlisted. We are not married and I am sitting here thinking, "great, he's going to go to Europe, and I am going to sit here in New York. That's good; that's healthy for a relationship, sure." So I picked it up and said, "all right, you want to talk?"

As he's talking, I am reading through this thing. I got the gist of everything I needed to know. I put it down and I am sitting there looking at him, and he's got a whole pile of them in his back pocket because he knows nothing will get by me unless I have all the information. So he is sitting there, and he says, "we can go to Europe, we can do this," and he keeps pulling brochures out of his back pocket, and I am like, "have you thought about this for a long time? This is not something you came home from lunch with." I said, "why didn't you say anything?" We talked about it, and his position was that he could get the Montgomery GI bill, he can get an education, he can learn a trade, and his ex-wife can't go after him for any of it. It's not like he is going to school to make more money so that he has to pay more child support when he gets a better job. The Army doesn't work like that. They don't pay you great, and we knew that. They don't pay you great until you start getting up there and you put years in. But his point was if he can't go to some kind of trade or technical school and he can't get a job on what he knows, jack-of-all-trades, then he needs to either refine those skills or to learn a whole new skill. And he gets $30,000 for college, and life insurance, and medical.

I said "well, that's all well and good, but I get jack. I don't get nothing. And on top of that, I lose a good job, because I guarantee you they are not going to station you in Brooklyn at Ft. Hamilton." I said, "we will end up somewhere in the middle of Kansas with Dorothy and the Scarecrow."

OFF TO BASIC TRAINING

I can tell you, the morning he left my house at 4:22 on a Thursday morning to go to basic, I was strong. I wasn't going to cry in front of this guy. I wasn't going to make him feel bad that he was leaving. I know he needs to do this; I am right behind him; I am going to be supportive; even if I am going to cry, he is never going to see it. Well, when I saw the little red Dodge Aries K pulled up and the recruiter picked him up, we walked down those stairs, that man was doing pushups in our driveway at 4:15 in the morning. I thought, "there is somebody who needs another prescription." He pulled out around that corner, and I walked up those stairs, and I sat on that couch, and I cried. I stopped crying because I didn't know what that sound was, and I sat in that dark living room trying to figure out what is that noise, and I figured out that, my God, it was coming from me.

Everybody knew, my family and my friends knew, and my boss at work knew that he was leaving, and if [my boss] wanted anything, he had better ask for it before Thursday, because I am going to be barely useful Friday. You have got to give me the weekend, and I'll get through it. I can get through it in three days. I can work through the anger and the disappointment and loneliness in about three days. I'm good like that. By Monday, I'll be fine. Well, he calls from the airport, and I wasn't home, and when I got home and I heard the answering machine tape, I fell to my knees. I was a 31-year-old adult, and I am hitting the floor. I still have the tapes. I saved all the letters I got from basic, the tapes, everything, all his pictures. I saved everything. It's in a box, about this big, and he doesn't know about it. He doesn't know I saved any of it. I saved the maps from when I went down there for graduation. I saved the pictures, I saved everything. I saved a copy of the car rental from when I came down here.

His basic [training] was eight weeks. His [additional skill training as a] heavy wheel mechanic was nine weeks. He said, "after 17 or 18 weeks, I'll be home." I think we figured out he'd be home the week of Christmas. Yeah right. That was when we found out the Army only worked on "ish" time. When they are ready. Five-ish, six-ish weeks, seven-ish weeks. We didn't know. They told him, "Well, we didn't have enough people in class, you guys will sit here until we get enough." He spent three weeks in holding waiting for people to get in this class. So he was kind of fired up, but his 17 weeks of basic and AIT were 28 weeks.

And here I was pushing a January wedding to a February wedding to a March wedding. We ended up getting married in March. We married on March 16. I brought him to JFK International Airport on March 17 and shipped him down here to this lovely piece of heaven.

He had come and gone on the plane for Christmas and New Years, he came home in February, and he came home to the wedding in March. Of all the times I had picked him up at the airport and brought him home and did all this stuff, when he left after we got married in March, that's the only time I cried. Our best man went with us. That was the only time Matt had volunteered to go was the day after the wedding, and I put Vic on the plane, and I turned around, and I had my head down because I didn't want Matt to see me crying. I still had my hair up in the horrible hair spray bride's thing, 96 bobby pins in there, I couldn't even find them all, and I just put my brand new husband on a plane, and his final words to me were, "Sweetheart, we'll have a honeymoon in Savannah."

WELCOME TO FT. STEWART

They lied. "Ft. Stewart is right by Savannah," they say. Yeah, 45 miles from Savannah. I'm telling you, this is the farthest I've ever lived from a mall in my entire life. I grew up in Long Island where you were eight miles from Roselle Field, the largest mall on the eastern seaboard. I live 46 miles from the Savannah Mall, which is like, what is that, a shopping center?

My sister-in-law is pregnant. She registered at Babies 'R Us, a Toys 'R Us branch affiliate. Everybody's got Toys 'R Us, right? I say, "that's great, because I'm sure I can find one down here." So we went to a Toys 'R Us, and I asked can I get a copy of a baby registry from Babies 'R Us and she said sure, no problem, and zips out nine pages my lunatic sister-in-law thinks she needs for her baby, and I turn around to leave, and then I stop and ask the lady where the nearest Babies 'R Us is and she says, "Charleston, South Carolina, or Jacksonville, Florida." I said, "oh, thank you."

FINDING A HOME

I flew down here. The best man and I flew down here, we rented this house, Matt and I. Vic was in the field at the time, and when he came out, we left the rental car for him and in the rental car was an envelope that said you now live here. I left the car rental agreement and the house keys and a map. The longest way around town that you could imagine to get from the post, right over there, to here, because I didn't know there was a back road. I can get you from 42nd Street; I can get you through Queens, Brooklyn, and Staten Island; but Hinesville, there are not enough people here for me to figure out where I am going. Nobody actually said base was here. They tell you take 119 to 196, take 196 to 38, up to 84. Go out Memorial Drive down to General Scrivener, at General Screen make a left on 119, to 84, take 84 until you see General Stewart, which is 38. I wrote these directions down. Now, my husband has been down here a month and a half, and he's been driving around with the guys, and he looks at this map. He must have died laughing. I got home that night. He calls up two days later and says "you know we live six blocks from the base," and I says "well it must be the back end of the base because you got to pack a lunch to get to the house." It's six blocks away. I didn't know how great that was. I figured it was a nice house; I opened the front door, and there is a fireplace, he'll love it. There were enough bedrooms, there was an Army room so I don't have green stuff all over my house, I have a room for Army stuff, and I don't care what you do in there as long as all the green stuff is not scattered all over my house. I'm military, but I shouldn't look like I live military.

When I first moved down here, we pulled into this driveway May 2. I had been up here two weeks prior to lease the house. The week before I got here, before he came home to get me, I think Vic slept on the floor in the living room because it was his house, and he didn't have to sleep in the barracks any more. He hated the barracks. We pulled in the driveway at 4:00 in the morning on May 2, with a 29 foot truck, a 2-and-a-half-year-old, a five-year-old, and a seven-year-old, and Vic's brother and sister-in-law from North Carolina. They were on the way. We picked up his brother and his family and said come on let's go, I need bodies, because we had up in New York my brother, sister, Bridget, and Matt. They helped us pack our house. All of this stuff was in four rooms, okay. To put it on the truck was great, but getting down here, we had nobody to help us, so we grabbed Wayne. We stopped in Fayetteville, said, hi, how are you doing, get in the car and follow. My car was on a trailer. It's about five hours if you do the speed limit. We got here, and at 4 o'clock in the morning you are so wired from driving. We started unpacking the truck, and we were trying to make it quiet, and I've got a two-year-old screaming because he wanted to help. I was opening boxes to get things to hand him to take inside because I didn't want him waking up the neighbors. Come to find out the next morning, [pointing to surrounding homes] that is an E-7, that's an E-7, that's an E-6, retired military over here, retired military over here, retired military over there. I'm surrounded by rank. I didn't realize I had moved into rank. I liked the house, and they told me $525. Where do I sign? I am paying $765 for four rooms in New York. Where do I sign?

GETTING BUSTED

We got here, he got here as an E-2 in March of 1997, he got E-3 in October of last year, and August 31, the first week of September, he got busted to E-2 again. He didn't make it to a formation on time, he was two minutes late, and they busted him. It depends on what battalion you are with. We have some hard asses.

We have an E-6 that's been riding him since the day he walked into the motor pool. His first day, he was fresh out of AIT. He is wet behind the ears, dripping. Just got out of AIT. He's still saluting everything that has got more than two stripes on it. Vic was, if not a buck private, damn near, and he walked up to her (a female E-6) and said I don't know if you do your service the same way I was taught. He's a heavy wheel mechanic. They are asking him to do service on a light wheel vehicle. He has no experience with this, none. Doesn't know who to ask, doesn't know who would know. His squad leader is not around, so he goes to the next in the chain of command, and she turns around and looks at him, and says, "well, get the book." Nobody has told him where the frigging books are. He says, "that's what I was going to ask you, was there a manual I could go through?" She goes over, grabs this thing, tome thing, you know, ancient paper, throws it onto the table and shoves it at him, and says, "can you frigging read?" That was his first day at the motor pool. He went home thinking "I didn't do something right in basic, because I didn't learn how to do this." And she has been riding him like the ponies since then, 18 months. Two weeks before she busted him her parting comment on Friday was: "I will make you a civilian, you will be a civilian."

She has a stick up her ass about my husband. I am a very type A personality. I am as high strung as they go. I am so allergic to change that it's incredible. I am not adaptable. My husband could stand at the motor vehicle department for three hours waiting for a signature and think nothing of it. If I stand in line three minutes, I'm freaked out. I have no patience. I am just type A, zipping around. My husband is so mellow, he's sensitive, easygoing. Whatever adversity he does encounter, he swallows. I think because he is quiet, mellow, and laid back, reserved, and not a squeaky wheel, that she feels either (a) he can't hack it, or (b) if he's going to take it, then I'm going to dish it.

The night he got busted, when he got home, I was sitting on the computer playing solitaire—another productive afternoon. He came in, and I heard the door open and close, and I heard him take his jacket off, and he came down the hallway, and you know those hats make noise when you throw them. "Whoosh." I looked at him and he's all red, but he is usually red. It was hot and sweaty. Took off all his stuff, threw the hat, threw the jacket, went in the bedroom, laid face down on the bed, and cried, and just cried. The only time I have ever seen him cry like that is when his ex-wife told him he wasn't allowed to see the kid, and he was visiting David through a fence when he was two and a half. He would sneak up to the house, and he would wait. He would sit across the street and wait for David to come out and play in the yard, and he would visit with his kid through the fence. That's the only other time I have heard him cry like that. I sat down on the bed with him and let him cry for a little bit, and then I said, "Honey you have to sit up; we have to talk." I said, "you can't do this." And he said, "I got busted."

He would sell his soul to make me happy, and I know that, and that's, when he came home busted that night, that's what I said to myself. "All right, he supports me all the time. He knows I hate the job. He knows I am miserable down here. He knows I had rather be working in a law office somewhere. He knows I hate the ride to Savannah. I just hate it; I can't do 40 miles and work for $6 to $8 an hour, which is what they are hiring for." I was making $19 and change in New York. It's a lot of work; it's hard work; it's a lot of head work, to work as a paralegal. You use logic and thinking and what ifs as a paralegal, but to do it for $6 or $8 an hour, I can't. That doesn't even pay for the stockings that you go through, you know what I mean? So as much as I would like to be a paralegal, it is not going to happen, at least not at this point.

I have one of the town's crappiest jobs right now. I work in a laundromat in town. There is no air conditioning; there are 24 gas dryers; there are 56 washers. I also do wash and fold. When the Guard comes in and they go into the field, there are some nasty things I got to wash, okay. Nasty things that I wouldn't give my husband to wash out for me, and these are people I don't know handing me these nasty things. Yes, it's sick, and it's minimum wage, and it's a nasty job, but I make my own hours. I go in when I want to. I go home when I want to. I work as many hours a week as I want. I sleep, I mop, and I hand out quarters. That's about the extent of it, outside of the wash and fold. As long as the Guard is gone, I don't do wash and fold very often now. But I had told him that as soon as he gets E-4—which was due in November, so this is actually a two-rank bust—or when we get housing, because we are on the eternal list for housing, I'll quit the job. But until then, we need it. It is $780 a month just to turn the lights on in this house, between the rent and everything else, and that doesn't include food and gas and recreation. That's just basic bills.

He brings home $1,079 base pay, $230 in separate rats, $431 in housing. My rent is $525 plus gas, plus electric, plus water, plus cable and phone. I have no choice but to work. Either that or we have to start selling drugs or stealing. There is no way around it. Prostitution, whatever is available, but I have to work. I have promised him, because he knows I am completely miserable with this job. I mean completely and thoroughly miserable at this job.

The boss is next door. She works in a convenience store, Flash Foods, next door to the laundromat. She comes over once in a while and breaks my chops. Today she brought in a blower, one of those electric blowers, so I can blow the dirt in the parking lot. She says, "why don't you sweep the parking lot." I didn't. I mean, what are you going to do, fire me? Somebody ran over a cat, I guess last night, because there is a dead cat in the parking lot. I got to work at 8:30 this morning and by 9:15, she is standing there saying, "you are going to have to do something with that cat." I said, "I ain't going to do shit with that cat. I don't have a cat, don't like cats, I am allergic to cats, didn't kill the cat, and don't deal with roadkill." I got my soda and walked out. I came back a little while later getting another refill of my soda and she said "what are you going to do about that cat?" I said, "I'll call DPW,[5] and if they don't do anything about it or the town doesn't do anything about it, it will just waste away there because I ain't doing nothing with that cat. It is not my problem. I didn't run the damn thing over, and I'm not going to clean anything up. I don't care what happens to the damn cat." I knew it was one of

---

[5]Department of Public Works.

the strays. We have strays at the laundromat, and they are mean cats. No skin off my back. I am really not an animal lover. Okay, I'm not. I never had animals as a child. I was allergic to them. My father was horribly allergic to them, and so was my brother. My sister and my mother used to fight us because we were allergic to them. But hey, you want me to inhale, take my next breath, don't get a cat. Get a cat, and you just lost three people. I have a fish tank. I have a 29 gallon aquarium. There are the pet lovers and there are the whatever. I am one of the whatever. I called the town and told them we had a dead cat in the parking lot, and she asked for my name, phone number, address, the whole nine yards and said okay and hung up. I'm not doing with this cat. This is a minimum wage job. You want something more than minimum, you have to pay for more than minimum.

When I tell you, it is the world's worst job, this is not an understatement, okay? And now that he's busted, and I know he is upset about it, I can't complain. He was in tears that afternoon. I have never seen him sob that hard in my life, over anything other than his son.

And I was upset. My first thought is he's busted, and I lose a $100 and change out of the check a month. That means I have to work. Now I have to. I was looking forward to no job in January. I was looking forward to unemployment.

FINANCIAL ISSUES

I had worked so hard for so long that I decided I was not going to work for a year when I got here. Based on the fact that the house [here] was only $525—the Army was paying all but $3 of the rent in New York, they paid $762 worth of housing in New York—so I figured that they would pay $525 down here. But our housing allowance is only $431.00. We are on a balanced budget for electric. It's $58 balanced. In the summer, you can easily run $110 a month or $150 a month. Water is between $32 and $45 a month. That includes sewer and garbage. Basically, it takes $780 a month to run this house, and that doesn't include food, gas, or cigarettes. It's staggering. Have

Table 4.1   Toni's Typical Monthly Pay Statement ($)

Pay	Base pay	1,079.00
	BAS (separate rations)	230.33
	BAH (housing allowance)	431.12
	Total pay	1,740.45
Deductions	Federal tax	13.67
	Social security	66.90
	Medicare	15.65
	State tax (NY)	11.58
	Life insurance	16.00
	AFRH	0.50
	Dental	20.00
	Child support	216.67
	Total deductions	360.97
Allotments	Additional Life Insur.	21.00
	Total Allotments	21.00
Monthly military income		**1,358.48**
Total monthly income (incl. her income)		**1,858.48**

NOTE: Pay statement does not yet reflect his recent "bust" to E-2.

Table 4.2   Toni's Monthly Bills ($)

Rent	525.00
Electric	58.00
Gas	75.00
Water	38.00
Cable	35.00
Phone (incl. Internet)	50.00
Car	—
Car insurance	53.00
Car Maintenance	20.00
Gasoline	50.00
Car registration	6.00
DPP [UCDPP]	30.00
Cigarettes	160.00
Total monthly bills (not including groceries)	**1,100.00**

you seen his take home pay? Don't tell me I can't work magic. [See Tables 4.1 and 4.2.]

Even still, I didn't get a job just because we needed the money. I got a job because I was going out of my mind. I got here in May. He got his 10 days [of leave]; he went back to work; and it was okay the first month because you are unpacking and putting things away, cleaning, you are doing all that fix-up-the-household thing. About August, I was stir crazy. I found myself standing at the back door, looking out the window, and every car that came up, I would think it was Vic pulling up in the driveway.

We went to Wendy's one night, right about that time, and he didn't realize that something was going to crack. All he knew is that when he came home, I was right up his ass. I was in his BDUs, asking what did you do, who did you talk to, what'd you say, what did you learn, etc. I mean right up his ass. And he thought I was interested in what he was doing. This is my wife, she is supporting my career. He was doing that man thing. My ego, a big head. What he didn't realize was that I was on the edge of losing my mind, okay. Because about 5:30 I am at the door, where the hell is he. Dinner was always ready, and the house was always sparkling, but there is only so much you can cook and do. One evening, I think it was five days straight I had been doing that, and I only realized I had been doing it five days straight once I fell apart.

[I finally fell apart] one night standing in Wendy's. He's standing next to me. "What do you want?" And I don't know why, but my eyes filled up with tears, and I just fell apart. I had a nervous breakdown in front of this poor little 17-year-old cashier in Wendy's, and she looked at me and just as he said what do you want, she said, something in her southern drawl that I couldn't translate, which was probably what pushed me over the edge, and I just stood back, and I said "I want to go hoooooome." That's it. I was at max capacity, fuses popping, that's it, I was done. The circuit breakers were popping. I was done. He had no idea that it was coming. You probably could have pushed him over like that. He was so shocked. He didn't know whether to hold me or back the hell up. This poor little cashier took one step backwards and just stood there. The manager working the grill looked at me. I looked at all of them, and I just fell apart, and I got in my car, and I just sat. It was my little Calgon moment, okay. I got in the car and I just sat there. Tears coming down. Wasn't blubbering or anything, just tears coming down my face, and I just sat there. And he gets in the car, and he sits there. And he says, "I don't know what to say." He joined the Army so he can make a life for us. My father told him straight to our face, when we told him we were getting married—not my father, my mother—said, "I don't think it is a good idea. He will never be able to support you like you are accustomed to. You'll have to work the rest of your life," okay, which was a stab in his heart, okay. He was also brought up, to know "you are going to support a wife someday. Learn to do something where you can support a wife." He joined the Army because he was working three jobs and getting nowhere in any of them, so he joined the Army to get a talent. $30,000 for college in four years. He thought, "I can do this. I will have some kind of a skill when I get out, I'll be all right." He sat there, and I think at that moment, he thought, "I'll quit the Army. If that's what she wants, if that's what's making her so upset, I'll quit." Because he is thinking that he is doing everything possible to make a life for us, to make me happy, you know. He sat there and saw me fall apart, and he was all ready to quit. He was ready to hang up his boots and go. He hasn't even been in a year yet. After I got my mind back, we talked and I was okay.

The next morning he gets up and goes to PT,[6] comes home, and I told him that I was getting a job, a part-time job, so now I am looking around. I started out 14 years old, working part-time at Wendy's. I really don't want to work in Wendy's. I found out the jobs on the base are, for the most part, unavailable. There are two- and three-year waiting lists to get into the commissary, or to get into the PX.[7] It is incredibly difficult. If you want to be a dishwasher at the Marne Club, that's open. If you want to be a waitress at the Marne Club, that's open, and of course it's the shift of 11 to 0-dark-30 that is open. The economy here is horrendous. That's when I found out the economy is horrendous. So, okay, can't get a job on base.

My friends kept telling me to volunteer. Most volunteers get picked up for work. Well, that's all well and good, except if I am going to work, I am getting paid for it, okay. Volunteerism wasn't a big priority in the work ethic in my family's philosophy. Volunteer my

---

[6]Physical training (a daily regimen in most units).

[7]Post Exchange.

ass, right after you pay me for it, okay. My position is that all skills are marketable. Somebody will pay for everything. I am not really good with the medical field, okay. I pass out watching my own blood come out of me, whether it's medically necessary or oops I slipped, so the hospital is completely out of the question, which leads me to the economy. Now, the economy is geared towards a transient population. It's a lot of fast food places; it's a lot of porn shops and bars. None of the places that I really want to go to work at.

[So I found the job at the laundromat] I make my own hours, I can work up to 40 hours a week. I said fine, I'll take it, okay. In the beginning, it was all right, until the weather got to the 103 and 106 and 113 degrees, and there are eight triple-sized washing machines in there, 24 dryers, and 48 little washers. The heat in there that would build up is horrendous, and it is a wash-and-fold laundromat. The National Guard came in April. National Guard are the laziest sons-of-bitches in green. They came in for two weeks, they go to the field for probably 11 out of those 14 days, and those three days they come out of the field, they bring their laundry up to get it cleaned. At one point, I had 19 loads of laundry to do in one day. I'm washing out-of-the-field underwear. I am folding other people's socks. There were things I would open up the bags, and it would curl my hair. There was stuff I wouldn't touch. Just open the bag, and shove the whole damn bag in there, shove it out of the bag and then put the bag in too. I never washed my hands so much in my life. I don't mind washing my husband's underwear, but I am washing other people's underwear and stuff, and that's pretty gross. And what's worse, there are females who bring clothes in, okay. Not for nothing, when I first got my period, my mother always said if you have an accident, cold water. I don't think every mother in the world ever told her daughter that. This is where I am working, okay.

When I first took it over in May, we needed the money. It got to the point where I had to pay my father back, and he had called me one day. I had started working 8:30 to 2:30 because that was about as long as I could stand the heat. That was earliest I could manage to get my butt there, and it was the latest I could manage to stay there. My father called me one day, just to say hi. I had just got home from work, and I had had a crappy day, with nasty Guard underwear. Dad says, "so quit, what's the problem?" I said, "I got too many bills, Dad, and I owe you money." He said, "I didn't ask you for the money back." So right there that was a load off. I still feel a moral obligation to pay it back, but it's not like I have to send him money to do it now. When I get it, I get it.

Still, I can't quit now. I told Vic I would quit the laundromat when he got E-4 and we moved into housing. We are number 211 on the list. And he's gotten busted. It doesn't change our place on the list. It's the same as the list for E-3. But E-4 is on a different list. Then it's the next day. You hit E-4 and you move into housing. That was another reason he got so upset when he got busted was that he knew I am miserable at my job, that I would quit when he hit E-4, and that's not going to happen, okay. No problem. We are number 211.

Her Pregnancies

We got married in August, he left in September. He came back in March after AIT. I spent April packing the house in New York. He came back the last weekend in April. It was May when we put our stuff on a 29 foot truck and drove down here. It was just before Memorial Day last year I figured I was pregnant. I think I was about 7 or 8 weeks. I miscarried on the Fourth of July of last year. The doctor said I was about 11 and a half weeks. I was three days shy of them letting me make an appointment. They won't let you make an appointment until you are 12 weeks. I miscarried the Fourth of July weekend. They told me, give yourself a break, wait a couple of months, and get pregnant again.

I got pregnant again. Didn't know it. I was on the pill. Didn't know I was pregnant until the week before Thanksgiving, November 17, and at that point, I was pretty pregnant, okay. I had nine people coming for Thanksgiving. I had a 20 pound bird in the oven, and I am gagging over the smell of turkey. So I was five-and-a-half months pregnant when I went to New York at Christmas. When I got there, it was two days before my father's birthday. His birthday is December 29, and my mother made an appointment at my GYN[8] because she wanted to hear the baby's heartbeat because she was not going to be down here for the baby's birth. This was the only time during the pregnancy that she was going to be able see me and to have anything to do with this baby. We didn't know yet that there were any problems with the baby. I had only been to the doctor two weeks prior, and they did the blood tests and the ultrasound and all this other stuff, and nobody gave me any results. They said 10 to 14 days and give us a call. Well those days fell when we were up in New York.

I got my whole family there at the doctor's with me. I got ten people and a doctor and me on a table with my stomach sticking out, and he's got this gel with the ultrasound thing, trying to pick up the baby's heartbeat. They recorded the baby's heartbeat. Everybody is all excited. I am the oldest child. "Oh, she's having a baby, we'll have our first grandchild." This is my grandmother's 14th great-grandchild. She had four kids, 12 grandchildren, and 14 great-grandchildren. This is number 14. And my father, on his birthday, sat in Wendy's with his little old retirement klatch saying "this is my grandson—listen to my grandson, listen." He was just all excited about it.

During the time I was in New York, I called here to check the messages and saw that there were seven messages. Every day the hospital had called, trying to get me to go down and have tests redone. So I called the hospital. There was nothing they could do over the phone. The lady who would tell me what was going on was gone, so I had to wait until I got back. I got back on January 5, and I went down and they redid the tests, and they told me that the tests came up as either something was terribly wrong with this child, because the blood results were off the scale, the fetal protein that is only supposed to be in the baby's amniotic fluid was so high in my bloodstream that they ran the test twice to make sure what they had, thinking that they might have screwed it up.

They told me that the baby had horrible amounts of protein in my bloodstream, which indicated neural-tube defects. They were telling me severe, not just he is going to walk with a limp, we are talking we don't know if he is going to walk at all. We don't know if he

---

[8]Gynecologist.

will have bladder control. Then they told me that the cerebellum, the back of the baby's brain, was missing, and I am like, wait a minute, where in the hell did this come from? You are telling me neural-tube defects. What they don't tell you is that neural-tube is part of the brain and the brain stem that goes down through the spine, and you don't realize, when you speak of neural defects, you are also speaking of anencephally, which is failure for the brain to develop, okay.

After my appointment I spent three hours at Liberty County Library going through Gray's anatomy. I had medical books and encyclopedias and anatomical encyclopedias open, and I am making notes on all this. What are they talking about; what are the possibilities—I wanted to know everything. I don't want to sit here and listen to people "yes" me. They treat you a lot like you are an 18-year-old, like you don't need to know. It just annoyed the shit out of me. I wasn't getting enough information, and here they are telling me that it is potentially a genetic thing, and I am sitting there thinking, wait a minute, Vic has a healthy son, he's got two brothers and a sister, and they each have two or three kids, and there is nothing wrong with them. But you know, my sister and I have no children, and you are telling me this is genetic.

My cousin is a neonatal pediatrician. Her husband is a neonatal respiratory physician. She has had a problem having children. She just adopted her second little baby boy and was at the birth and cut the cord and the whole nine yards. Lynn tried in vitro and all kinds of stuff, and it didn't work, so I got home and called Lynn and I had all these test results and the numbers, and when I told her the numbers, she said "oh Toni." The numbers were off the scale. They were so bad, they were off the scale, and I had to sit there and make a decision, look what it comes down to, it is (a) being a military wife, if you are going to have a family, it's you against them; you can't depend on the fact that your husband is going to be there 24 and 7, 365.[9]

They told me straight up that they would induce me at eight months, and they couldn't guarantee that the child would live two minutes, two hours, two weeks, two days, two years, they didn't know. I would never be able to hold the baby. I would never be able

---

[9] 24 hours a day, 7 days a week, 365 days a year.

to touch him. They would deliver it C-section and hook him up to tubes and wires and the baby would be in an isolette until it died. But on the good side, as far as Tricare was concerned, they would have a priest there for me, they would make sure all the burial arrangements were together.

No, I couldn't do it. No way. You are not going to do this to my son. I'll give this child back to God before I will give him to you to do that to him. That's not fair. He hasn't felt any pain yet. I am not going to let you do that to him.

It's you against everybody else. It's my family versus everything else. All the ills in the world, all the evil in the world, it's me against them. If I am going to have a handicapped child, a baby boy, it's going to be me doing it. Now, I know I can count on Vic when he is here, but if they deploy him to Bosnia for nine months, or if the Persian Gulf crisis turns into a full-fledged war, what am I going to do? I am going to saddle myself with something. What am I going to do? In the event he doesn't get deployed, and there is no war, if you have a severely handicapped child, you end up in the exceptional child program, which is a good program. It's a brilliant idea. I'm glad the Army came up with it, but it cuts your career choices down. Having this handicapped child puts you in a position where the duty stations open to you are based on what medical facilities are available for that child. I don't want to do that. I don't want to stop his career. He told me in the beginning, yes, it is our child; yes, it is our decision; but it is something you have to decide. He says I got you here, and I will stand with you no matter what you do, and when I tell you he stood in every procedure except the final procedure, he stood through every one of them. He stood when they injected me with the needle and put the digitalis in the infant. He stood there through sonograms. He stood there through amnio. He stood there through ultrasound, and I sat there, and I looked up at him, so I wouldn't have to see anything going on. I would just look at him and the two of us would just sit there and silently cry, and you would see the tears coming down.

Tricare wouldn't cover [the termination]. I would have to be on a transplant list to get the Army to pay for it, and I sat with the health and benefits advisor, and it is specifically written in Tricare's rules and regulations, they will not pay for abortion services for the following conditions regardless: Anencephally, neuro or neural-tube defects, psychiatric—here are like five things they won't pay for, and I had two of them. The only reason they would pay would be that if it endangered the life of the mother or if the mother was on a transplant list, heart-lung transplant. I would have to have a major organ transplant; a broken arm ain't going to cut it. And I actually told the health benefits advisor just before I walked out of her office, and she thought I was going to commit suicide because at that point I had said it so many times, five-and-a-half months pregnant, the baby has anencephally and spina bifida; the AFP in my blood is off the scales; I have gone through sonograms, been through genetic counseling, [etc.].

So I called my father and I said "Daddy, I need money." I had talked to my parents about it, and I had asked my mother that whole week prior to making the final decision. I said, "Mommy, what would you do?" My mother worked for an OB/GYN, and that OB/GYN did the planned parenthood, the local planned parenthood abortions, so I know that she has never been anti-abortion, okay, but that is not the point. This is your kid, this is your daughter, and this is your grandson, and we knew it was a boy.

She told me straight out. She said, "Toni, I'd terminate. Honey, you have to understand. Your husband is in the military." And she thought the same way I did—the apple doesn't fall far. "Your husband is in the military. It's not going to be both of you forever, it is going to be just you." She said, "you have had back surgery, your back's been hurting for two years now, you are not going to be able to lift this child, you are going to have to change this baby's diaper until this baby is in his forties, if he lives that long." They already told me that if I did go through with the entire pregnancy, they would induce me at seven months, C-section me, hook the baby up, tubes and wires, and EKGs and tubes. They said because of the anencephally, they weren't entirely sure that the baby would live. They couldn't say how long he would live. But what they were sure of was that they would have induced me, put it in an isolette, hooked it up with all these wires and everything else. I would never have been able to touch him. I would have never been able to hold him. They would have made sure that there were not only the OBs in the delivery room but there would have been neonatal specialists and they would have made sure that there was a priest on site for me, to give last rites to the baby, and they would make sure [to] make arrangements for the funeral services. I could pick out the casket, etc.

You listening to me? This is supposed to be a baby's birth, and I'm listening to them talk about picking out a casket and a christening outfit, and I can't do this. And what's going through my mind is a tiny casket, and I can't do this. And meanwhile, they are telling me this kid is never going to move, never going to walk. Meanwhile, this kid is doing a watusi on my bladder. I tell you, this kid would kick me. I sleep on this side when I first go to sleep, but I wake up on this one. But I fall asleep on this one. Vic sleeps on the same side, so we are belly to back. The kid let out a kick, okay, woke him up. A week later, they are telling me the kid will never walk or never move on his own. His gross motor skills will be nonexistent because he doesn't have a cerebellum.

And they are sitting there telling me this, and I am telling them, "but I've got pictures." The ultrasound lady would say, "now let me see your fingers," and you know sometimes you have to poke them to get them to move, I've got pictures. They wanted to see if he had a cleft lip. He was perfect, he'd turn his head. "Let me see your behind," "your back," and the kid would turn around and show them his butt. You could count every frigging vertebrae. "All right, let's see if you are a boy or a girl." I've got pictures of all this, and you are telling me this kid is never going to move. I'm telling you this kid is doing the watusi on my bladder, you are telling me he is never going to move. Somebody is wrong here. And then they are telling me I have to pick out a casket. I can't do that. I am Roman Catholic. I grew up Roman Catholic. I know abortion is a sin, but you know what, I am not anti-abortion. I am pro-choice, and nobody I know can listen to what I had to think about and what I had to go through and tell me that they would not have done it.

My mother's birthday is January 19, and on January 19, we terminated the pregnancy.

Everybody in New York when I talk to them says, "well are you going to have a baby?" It's only September. All this happened in January of this year. They are ready now. As far as they are concerned, I am ready. My position is, "oh ye of little memory." Victor went through the whole thing with me. It's a two-day procedure. We had to drive to Atlanta, and it is a two-day procedure. And it is a very painful, very emotional, crappy thing to do on a weekend. He went through every single step, every single step with me, standing there holding my hands, and I would not look at anything else in the room but him through every procedure, and the final procedure was the only thing he didn't go through, which was obviously the worst of all of it.

Vic and I used to think that it was that we couldn't get pregnant. Then we figured out that maybe it was an incompetent cervix, maybe that's what it is. We just can't hold them. Nope, we can get pregnant. Getting pregnant ain't the problem. Holding the baby, no problem. It's making a good one, that's the problem. I am afraid to try to have another baby. See, it's a big moral, emotional conflict thing. I am going to have a problem.

Vic's been making peeps again about wanting a baby, and he first started, I'd say about the beginning of August. He won't come out and directly say. He doesn't pressure me. He doesn't push it, but he makes his point well known.

I don't know that he is thinking in terms of reality. I can't see us having a child. He's an E-2. Now, granted, he's only been an E-2 these two weeks. He's thinking in terms of the Army, a career, a family, and that. I am thinking that a family would be nice, but I am not going to wonder every month where the next diaper is going to come from because I don't have the money to pay for diapers, and I don't have the money to pay for formula, and I don't have the money for car seats and strollers and layettes and everything else and outfits every month because they are outgrowing everything. I can't do it. And I know that Vic and his first wife went through that. But she had her parents living downstairs. She could go downstairs and ask daddy. I don't have that luxury. My father pretty much told me straight up, "you do it on your own. Your mother and I did it on our own, you'll

do it on your own, and you will do anything you have to to do it."
And he's right. I did go to him for money once, already. He doesn't
throw it in my face. He was really good about it, but based on the
reason that he would never throw it in my face. He is not mean and
evil, and he understood. But I don't have that kind of luxury that Vic
had in his first marriage. I can't worry where our next meal is coming from, and I won't do that with an infant. I won't wonder how I
am going to feed this kid.

There is WIC, but surprisingly enough, WIC is not like something
you can get because you are pregnant. It has to do with your income.
Vic and I, last October just after he got his E-3, went to apply for
food stamps. Everybody else was walking around with food stamps
and they got Nikes and Air Jordans, $130 sneakers on. I am stand-
ing here with a safety pin holding my bra together, okay. They are
wearing Tommy Hilfiger, I am wearing Vic's old camp tee-shirts,
okay. Something is wrong here. So I went down and it turned out we
made $400 too much a month to qualify, and the lady who inter-
viewed us actually told us that as soon as you get housing and you
lose your [housing allowance], which was about $400, come back,
you are eligible.

FAMILY RELATIONSHIP

My brother and I had a fight on the phone a couple of weeks ago,
two weeks ago. It got to the point where Vic was in the bedroom and
he gets out of the shower, and he hears me screaming in the kitchen.
In the six years I have known Vic, he has never heard me raise my
voice to my brother. This kid is in Queens, New York, and I am
screaming from Georgia. I should have been able to open the door,
and you should have heard me. All because I finally asked who is
going to be the baby's godparents. I said, "Tom, who is the baby's
godparents going to be?" He said, "well, we are going to make it
Damien because Matthew is a plain old fuck-up, and he is still on
heroin." Jennifer's older brother is addicted to heroin, bad, and it's
been like this a lot of years, not a model godparent, not somebody
you want to stand up at church and, "yes, I do." As a matter of fact,

he was sober for the wedding ceremony, and promptly—right after the ceremony and after the pictures—he went out and tied one on, so he was loaded at the reception. And he is 18 years old, I mean 19 years old, sorry. So the godfather is Damien, the younger brother. He just turned 18. I said, "who is the godmother?" He says, "Pam, because she is closer." And I stepped back a second. Pam is my sister. I am the oldest, my sister is the middle, and then Tom is the baby. And I said, "oh, that will be great." He goes, "well she's just here and I don't know whether you are going to be in Germany for the next six years, I don't know where the hell you are going to be, and I want somebody who is going to see this kid and be with this kid, and I want this kid to know his godparents, and I don't know what the hell you are going to be doing, etc."

And then I got to the point, and I say, "Tom, are you saying that because I am in Georgia, I am not close to the family? Because that's what it sounded like." He goes, "yes." That lit my fuse. I was done. I said, "Okay. Let me just break a few things to you gently. First off, this is the fucking 90s, welcome to the age of airplanes. This is the Army, welcome to space A travel, you know." Well, he says, "I don't know if you are going to be in Germany. You talk about you want to go to Germany." I said, "yeah, I want to go to Italy and Japan too. Is that going to stop me from being part of this family because I am living in Georgia, and I don't live in the center of the fucking universe called New York, because I don't live within five minutes from you, I am not part of this family any more because I don't stop by." He told me I stopped by for Christmas, *stopped* by.

His point was, that I was not around any more. I am not part of the family any more. I am not close to the family. I got my own life. The family don't count. This is the way he thinks I look at it. I only stop by for Christmas. Another statement he made was when was the last time you came home? When was the last time I saw you? And I said Christmas. He doesn't want his kid to have absentee godparents, okay. My brother is very family-oriented. It really upset him a lot to see me leave. He cried at the reception. When the reception was over, we sang New York, New York, the whole nine yards. He got upset because I think, at that point, he realized I was out of there. He isn't going to be able to call Toni up, and she's going to be able to be one town away or whatever any more.

I didn't look at it as leaving the family. He looked at it that way. There are a lot of times that I am grateful I live so far away. It's not like my family is the model of dysfunctional, okay, but I didn't grow up walking the yellow brick road either.

But I think part of the problem I am having about going home is I want a kid so bad. I am going to have to go back for Christmas, and I really honestly think—and I have been thinking about this for a couple of days—I am going to cut the trip short, and I am going to tell them that Vic can't get that much leave. See, there are certain things that I can get away with because they don't know the military. I can't lie to another military family, but I can get over on the non-military. I just think it will be too hard.

HER FRIENDS

Anne is a good friend of mine.[10] She makes me laugh. I love her. I like people who make me laugh. I tend to make people laugh. I didn't know, when I first got here, I didn't know that you weren't supposed to talk to a command sergeant major's wife. You weren't supposed to be friends with a sergeant first class' wife.

It depends, though, on which colonel and which sergeant major are running the battalion. The last colonel we had, his wife, I used to call her the Ice Princess. The colonel's wife directs the air for the rest of the company, and her position, from what we understand as the underlings, there was no fraternization. If you were an E-2, you stayed with E-2, E-3, and E-4. That was it. Done. The wives wore rank. And then when the Ice Princess left, we got a new colonel in June.

A lot of us, before the Ice Princess left, a lot of us were rebelling against that. We would have socials, and it would be a bunch of wives who would get together once a month at the command sergeant major's house and the sergeant major would be relegated to go sit in the dining room and watch TV and his wife and maybe 12

---

[10]Anne is the battalion commander's wife.

of us from each of the companies—Alpha, Bravo, and Headquarters; my husband is in Headquarters Company—would sit around and we'd bitch about what our husband's were bitching to us about, and can you believe, and what do you do? It was mixed. Carol was the command sergeant major's wife. We had Lorraine, who was an E-7's wife; we had Amy, whose husband was an E-6; Belinda's husband is an E-6; a bunch of E-5s; and at the time, Janie and I were E-2s. But no officers' wives. Officer's wives are usually, well, you know.

Anne is a new generation. She is a year older than I am. She thinks on the same level as we do. She was born the same year as us. She was exposed to the same things we were. Whereas, a lot of the officers' wives are 45 and better, because they have already done most of their 20 years. And the lieutenants and captains, well, those are college lieutenants. They are younger. Those are the ones who came out of college. Those are not officers that went through the ranks. They didn't go in as an E-1. They went in as a Second Louie. There is a lot to be learned between E-1 and Second Louie. Our captain we just got in July started as a buck private, so he knows what it's like to be that kind of person. He forgets what it's like to live on that kind of money, though.

PROBLEMS IN THE UNIT

Our captain is not married. He has a three-year-old son, has a girlfriend, and has a sister who lives with him and does daycare for him, but I am the Family Support Group leader for the [Headquarters] Company.

My being Family Support Group leader doesn't affect my husband. Because what I do doesn't count for him. In the same light, what he does doesn't count for me. I have easier access to the captain [than he does]. I have easy access to the first sergeant. I could walk through the battalion and say, " Colonel Carson,[11] could I see you for a minute?" But the only reason I can do that is because I am Family Support Group leader, and what I have to say has to refer to that capacity. I can't go in there and say, "Daniello has a problem down

---

[11]The battalion commander.

in the motor pool, the sergeant is busting his chops, what are you going to do about it?"

We have a horrendous morale problem in the motor pool. The captain knows there's problems in the unit. The captain stood up in front of formation on Friday and he said, "straight up, man to man, I know there is a morale problem in this company, I don't know where the morale problem is coming from, I don't know what's going on, whether it's my NCOs, my E-1 through E-4s, whether it's my officers, I don't know what it is, but we got a morale problem because I have never seen so many people come to my office and ask for a transfer out of the company in my life." He's got officers asking to get the hell out, NCOs asking to get the hell out, E-1s through 4s asking to get out, everybody wants out.

Tonight Vic is bringing home another soldier who is having a problem with Sergeant Johnson in the same way that Vic is having it. Johnson is looking to bust her, and I've met her once or twice just in passing, hi, how are you, nothing one on one. She filed an EO[12] complaint. They bounced the complaint because they said it wasn't an EO complaint. Now she wants to talk to me and find out if I will help her file an IG[13] complaint. And I told Vic, I said I will talk to her, I will ask her if she has talked to Jim[14] yet, because that is her first route of attack. If you can't get your chain of command and nobody listens there, then go to Jim, and if you have to go to Jim's house, catch him in the parking lot, nail him at PT, whatever you have to do, but talk to Jim, because she wants to go to IG. I don't know that that is the right place to go, but I don't know what her problem is, so I told Vic, bring her to dinner tonight, tell her I got chili I made last night. I'll feed her, but I need to know what her situation is before I recommend anything. It's not like I can recommend jack, I'm an E-3's wife, I know from nothing about the Army, but I know what I've been through so far, and I know what routes I went through.

Every once in a while, Vic has people come over, work on my car, do this, help me do this, I'll have anywhere from two to six E-1s, E-

---

[12]Equal Opportunity.

[13]Inspector General.

[14]The command sergeant major.

2s, or E-3s sitting in my living room. You get to talking and cutting the shit with them. Most of what their problem is, when you cut out all the fat and get right to the meat, their direct superiors, their squad leaders, and their immediate NCOs are more likely to tell them, "your PT score sucks" rather than tell them, "hey, your PT score went up six points from the last one you took three months ago." They don't have any source of "atta-boys," none. Their NCOs are what they call ghost NCOs. You've heard of them; they give the order, and then disappear. That's what they get, and then all of a sudden they are back an hour later, saying "done yet?" And all that E-2 or E-3 wants to do is to smack him in the kneecap with a wrench, and say, "No, I am out here in 105 degrees, baking in the sun like a french fry, and you are in that office with your feet up in the air-conditioning, and you are going to ask me if I'm done yet."

The command sergeant major is a very good guy, actually. Once I had to call him because Vic was supposed to get an invitation at the motor pool through his motor sergeant, and his motor sergeant was holding it hostage for a check because he was supposed to pay for them, and what I was told through the battalion Family Support to let the wives know that these were coming home this weekend, that this was what it was about, this is how much it costs, etc. I didn't even get it. Now, here I am. I activated the damn phone tree. These wives are standing on the husbands' chest and on the hoods of their cars, "where's my invitation!" And Sergeant Johnson is holding them up as ransom. You give me a check, I'll give you an invitation.

So I had called, at that time I was the secretary of the Family Support Group, so I had called my FSG leader, who was an E-5 spouse. Her husband was also having a problem in the unit and was transferred out of the company into Alpha Company because he was having a personality conflict. So I called Connie. Connie says I don't know what to do with that, call Carol. Carol is the sergeant major's wife, and she is the advisor for the FSG. Now, at the time, Carol was walking to relieve stress, and she would walk five or six miles just to walk it out. So I called about 8:00. It's getting dark, she's got to be home now, and I get Jim, the command sergeant major, on the phone. And I says, "It's Toni, and how are you Jim, sweetie." ("Jim sweetie" makes my husband's skin crawl. "Jim sweetie" makes his eyes roll. But that's how we speak to each other.) And he says, "Is there anything I can help you with?" And I said, "Maybe. You know those invitations?" He says, "yeah, they were supposed to go out today; did you get one?" I said "no, it is being held hostage in the motor pool." So he promised me, "I'll care of it first thing, you'll have them by Monday by lunch, your husband will have it in his hands," and goddamn if it wasn't in his hand at lunch.

When you go to Jim and complain, he is really cool about it. I know this because as Sergeant Johnson was handing out these invitations, like she was supposed to do the Friday before, she said whoever went to the First Sergeant to complain about this ought to come to me first, because I don't want it coming down from the First Sergeant. It didn't come down from the first sergeant, it came down from the command sergeant major. Shit rolls downhill. I don't play with the little boys. I go right to the top. I don't want to play with the middle man. Our captain is not married, and our first sergeant is not married. Our motor pool sergeant is married, but his wife wants nothing to do with FSG.

Carol and Jim, the command sergeant major, if they could keep the sergeant major pay and go back to him being a first sergeant, they would do it in a minute. He would rather deal with the soldiers and that work than sit in the battalion and be so isolated from it and not know what is going on until it is blown up so bad it looks like Hiroshima. You know what I mean. It's not just a bucket of shit, it's a land mine. He would rather be doing that. So he tries to stay involved with the troops.

Like when they were working outside, Jim would be out there talking to the guys. A couple of times he caught sergeants and first sergeants, staff sergeants, and even lieutenants screaming at these guys—these E-1s through E-4s. They have never done this. They are supposed to be learning, and they are standing there on a 103 degree day, sweating their asses off, having to stay in uniform in case the frigging general walks by, and lieutenant jerky boy is yelling at this poor kid, so Jim came up at one point, and this lieutenant was ripping a new one into this E-3, and Jim just laid him out, told him how it was and how it was going to be. Told the E-3, "soldier go back to what you were doing. As a matter of fact, take 15, get some water, and then go back to what you were doing." He won't yell at you in front of anybody, but he pulled that lieutenant over and they knew he was ripping the lieutenant a new one for ripping that kid up in front of the whole damn company. He's never done this job. He is from middle frigging America. The kid may not have even lived on a road where he came from, and here you are trying to dig a trench. They are looking at books and doing it by the book, yep, literally. Step two, figure A. Jim told the lieutenant, "you are supposed to be training these guys," and Jim made the lieutenant get in there and do it. Jim's big thing is that he doesn't want his soldiers abused, and they were, we were, getting abused.

So anyway, recently they called Vic in on a Saturday. They told him on Friday night that they were to come into work on Saturday morning from 9 to 12, and you are done. During the course of that week, his boots ripped. Now, these are two-year-old boots. These are the first ones he got, you know, shave your head, here's your uniform, your boots, welcome to the Army. They are finally dead. The heels are history on them, chunks are missing out of them, they are starting to talk, the flap was ripped, so that every time he tied them you could still see his uniform through it. He needs to get boots. We were going to do that on Saturday afternoon.

He was told on Friday, civvies, from 9 to 3. They had to spray paint diamonds and numbers on seven trucks. Now keep in mind they don't know where these orders come from. All they know is that Sergeant Johnson, Betty Johnson—Uncle Betty they call her—Uncle Betty says these have to be done by Friday and if they are not done by Friday, they need to be completely done by Monday. So of course, seven trucks ended up by not being done. He was pissed that Friday because when he got home, he said I have got to work frigging Saturday because I got two sergeants sleeping under a frigging truck, and when I go up there and ask them can I start spray painting, at least get a couple done, they say, "no don't worry about it." So Uncle Betty turns around and says that the guys have to come in on Saturday, from 9 to 12. He gets home that night, on the machine it says, "09 to 1200, BDUs, click."

Before, he was not happy about going, but at least he was in civilians. Now he has to get into uniform. Not only that, but he's going to get paint on his uniform. He's got work clothes, ripped up jeans, jeans that we have painted three different apartments in that he could wear, now he's got to worry about getting paint on the uniform. Now he is twice as pissed as he was before. Wakes up Saturday, grabs a cup of coffee, goes. It's only three hours. The deal was that he was going to get home by 12:00 or 12:30, I'd have lunch for him, we'd hit the clothing and sales and get him the boots and stuff, Saturday is all planned out. Okay, so 1:30 Saturday afternoon, he's not home. I get a phone call. I say, "where the hell are you?" "I'm still here," he says. "They are making us do services on the trucks." Well, doing services is not spray-painting diamonds. I said, "honey, are you talking like tune-up service, semiannual, biannual, yearly service type stuff, or are you talking this truck died Friday night and it needs to be fixed by Monday?" He says no; oils and filters and put air in the tires, service, things that can wait until Monday.

Yes, now I am pissed off. Now, this is abusive. There is no reason to do this to them. The battalion lieutenant colonel keeps saying that we are in a period of sustainability. We are not under a deployment; the division is not being sent anywhere; we shouldn't be under any kind of pressure. So he says he doesn't know what time, so I said, "okay no problem."

Now I am getting calls from wives in the unit. "What's going on Toni?" A couple of them are brand new to the motor pool. They used to work at company, and the company is 9 to 5, in fact, if you're there at 5 after 5, you are late, you know. Now you are in the motor pool and they are working nights. They worked nights three times this week, and now it's Saturday, so these wives are upset. And I'm to the point where I am not lying to these women any more. I am not telling them it's all right. I said, you want to know how it is? Okay, you are not going to make dinner every night and expect everyone to have a sit-down meal. You are going to make dinner that you can put in Tupperware and you are going to buy plastic forks and spoons.

This weekend thing is brand new. I can't tell you anything about that, but I can tell you about Monday through Friday. I said, you keep telling me I've lost weight, I look great. I can tell you I haven't had a meal with him more than twice within the past three weeks.

So Saturday, I am fielding phone calls from wives asking why their husband is not home. Like I'm going to say he's at my place, playing poker (laugh). I don't know. I don't run the company, but I can tell you, my husband is down there too. I said it's not like they pulled out just some of them. Then I come to find out when he gets home at 4:20, that all he had all day was his cup of coffee. They sent the meal card holders to the chow hall at 12:00. They came back at 1:30. Married soldiers didn't get to eat. It's 4:20. They just worked 7-1/2 hours with no food.

This was the max. This really pushed me over the edge. See, Johnson will say meal card holders—because she believes that if you are a meal card holder you don't have anybody else to cook for you except the mess hall—go eat. "Spouses, your wife has got a warm pork chop sandwich at home, don't you worry about it." And that was the quote: "warm pork chop sandwich at home."

And after a year of her, the guys know that the more they complain about going home, the longer she keeps them. To the point where at times they would hang out sitting there waiting to be dismissed 45 minutes or an hour and a half. When this colonel took over in June, he found out that they had been waiting in the motor pool 45 minutes or so to be dismissed, hanging out, because they can't leave until somebody says go home. The colonel told the E-7s, all the motor pool sergeants, that if he found anybody hanging out and sitting there waiting to be dismissed, that he will dismiss them and he will stand there, and when the sergeant comes out to dismiss them, the colonel will be waiting for him. That scared them. And this colonel actually showed up at the motor pool.

FAMILY SUPPORT GROUP

Thanks to my big mouth, I'm now leader of the company Family Support Group.

When I took over the Family Support Group, a lot of the people who had stopped coming, who I knew personally, and I knew their husbands, I'd see them at the PX. Fourth of July, we had the fireworks, and I sat with one girl I hadn't seen in two months. [I asked her], "Megan, where have you been?" And she said, "Toni, I don't go to those things anymore; they are just a pain in my ass." And the more senior wives, some of them, not all of them, are snooty. Some of them couldn't be bothered. And in the beginning, I thought that's the way it is, and I have since learned through Carol, the command sergeant major's wife, that it's not supposed to be like that. The officers' wives and the NCOs' wives are supposed to be the wealths of information that should help the newbies get through all this and to get through the first deployment, to get through reunions, to show us how to cope through the deployment when they are gone. I don't have very many in my FSG. The ones who do show up, they are all E-4 and E-5, E-3 and E-2s. Since June, when I became the leader, the ones who have showed up lately are simply the ones that are my friends from before I was anything, when I was just sitting there like one of them.

I am having a hard time with the company FSG. When I took this over on June 30, I knew from experience that the hardest part of being the Family Support Group leader was that you fight with the company commander a lot. You don't get support from the company. If you're not getting support from the guys, you can't get support from their wives. Okay. So I knew that going in, so I was prepared for that. I had to give a copy of this phone list to our company commander because I have so many disconnects. Divorce, disconnects, and no phones. So either they moved; they lost the service; they changed the number for some reason. But the number we got is not good. On August 12, I updated this. On the 16th of September, we initiated the phone tree, and this was what I got back. Within two hours of my five phone calls, this was the responses I got back. I'm responsible for 65 names total. I had four disconnects, two PCSs,[15]

---

[15]Permanent Change of Station (a move to another Army post).

one mean person, another disconnect, a divorce, a disconnect, a retired. I also have three that don't speak English.

What I was told and what I've seen, is that the Family Support Group has no support from the company, from the soldier end. If you could get hold of the wives on your own, you got the support. But if you ask the company commander to put out a formation notice of a bake sale, a car wash, a hot dog sale, whatever, it might get there, it might not, it might be the correct information, it might be the right date, the right time, it might get home to the wives. Ninety percent of the time it does not.

We got a flier out in the mail for spouses' night out, and I made eleven phone calls to eleven people that I know, just to spot check and see what happened. Ninety percent of the soldiers have it in their cars. It never got to the house. I also made the spot check because he [the captain] gave it out the night before. We printed this thing up two weeks prior, brought it to him, and asked him if he could hand this out at formation tomorrow, and he said yeah, yeah, no problem. He handed it out Thursday, and the damn thing was Friday. The problem is he doesn't understand that spouses just don't sit on their ass and do nothing. We work. We have to change daycare; we have to change meals; we have to move things around. If we want to go out and spend five minutes with adults, we have to make concessions in life. Feed the husband; feed the family; feed everything; then get in the car. These are the things we have to do. This commander just don't get it. He thinks all these wives do is sit down and eat bon-bons and watch Married with Children. He's not married. You know, I am just trying to get it past this guy. We don't make enough money to live. Most of us are living on the economy, and most of us can't swing it. You can't ask these girls to take a day off. You can't ask them to change their schedules. We can't do it.

What I am also finding out, and I just found this out last week, is that the low morale in the company affects the FSG. We were going to have a bake sale on Wednesday. We activated the phone tree Friday, Saturday, and Sunday, and the response I got went from icy cold to sure, how much do you want me to make, you know, and for the majority of them, a lot of them were not very interested.

Anyway, bottom line, the next Wednesday, this was around September 13 that they did that Saturday. On the 16th we had a bake sale. Those 60 people on that phone tree that I just showed you? I called my five girls and told them to call their phone tree. I asked them to initiate this phone tree on Friday, Saturday, and Sunday, depending on who I got on what day. Bake sale on September 16th, Organization Day on October 16, Halloween party coming up at the end of the month, and we have a meeting on the 6th. I am not going to initiate the phone tree and tell them just one thing and then call every week telling them something. That's a pain in the ass. I don't want to hear from people that often. My deal is you call everybody on your list, and the last person on the list calls me and tells me what you were told, so I know if it's a game of telephone or if you are getting the proper information.

Bake sale shows up that Monday. This is the Monday after Vic worked all day Saturday at the motor pool. Since I am getting a hard time at work taking off time in the afternoons, the deal was I was going to leave there at 9:30, set the thing up in front of the PX, get the tables. Captain Northway[16] was going to bring the baked goods in the back of his truck. The soldiers were supposed to bring all the baked goods from their homes in the morning of the bake sale to PT, put it all in the orderly room. Northway would pile up his truck and bring it up to the PX. So I asked him look, I've got a pregnant woman, a woman with a bad back, and I can't stay there all day, I need some help. He gave me four soldiers—two girls, two guys. I got everything from an E-3 to an E-6. No problem. He backed me up. (It was kind of shocking. So he is backing me, right. I noticed it, but I didn't say anything. I still make him call me Mrs. Daniello, not Toni, Mrs. Daniello—(a) I am older than him, and (b) I am not enlisted. When I join the damn Army, he can call me Toni.)

So it is 9:40, and I am looking at my watch. Where the hell is the captain? I have got five plates on this table. Big long table. The second table is set up next to it. Five things: two sets of brownies, choco-

---

[16]The company commander.

late chip cookies, Reese's pieces cookies, and a pistachio nut cake, like a Bundt cake. He told me 9:30. I'm thinking, where the hell is he? It's 20 to 10. Supposed to start this thing at 10:00, he's killing me, what's going on? The E-6 is looking at me and said, "what's going on, what are you waiting for?" I said, "where is your captain, he is supposed to be here at 9:30 with the rest of the baked goods. He is supposed to take them from the orderly room and put them into his truck and bring them here by 9:30." All four of the soldiers said, "that's all that was in the orderly room." I just sat there. Five baked goods. I have gotten fired from better jobs than this. I stood there. It wasn't so much that I felt like I had been punched in the chest, but I was instantly angry. I was talking about chocolate chip cookies to people that I don't want to talk to normally, at 10:30 on Sunday night. I am leaving for Orlando in 18 hours. I got five frigging things for a bake sale. I ran around for two weeks talking to people on this base getting permission, scheduling things, making sure I could get the tables, making sure I could get the authorization, getting cash, setting the change box up with $40 out of my pocket. Drew a sign at 11:30 the night before because the sign that we had from the last one is gone, and I am standing here looking at four soldiers, two wives, and only five plates.

I have five people bring stuff out of the 60 people on that phone tree, and it was put out at formation. I was angry. I was embarrassed. I was humiliated. And my first thought was, they are not going to break me. You are not going to break me. And I looked at Jody and she's seven months pregnant. I whipped money out of my pocket. I handed her $20 and said "commissary. Go get some cookies, zip locks and tape." I handed Jenna another $20 and I said "donuts." Behind me the Chaplain's housekeeper pulls up and she opens her car and she's got cookies and stuff that she baked, so now I got maybe ten trays: two cakes she's got, and cookies and stuff. And I said thank God for Sue. She annoys the hell out of me, but thank God for Sue. Jody comes back. They bought Oreos and Chips Ahoy, and brownies and whatever was there, and we are fixing little baggies and we are just spreading it out.

Bottom line, after all this, I went back to work after 11:00. I paced back and forth. I have a little office at the laundromat. I am angry. This is not a paying job. I got 60 people that knew about this damn bake sale and five items. I didn't ask you to make anything from scratch. I wasn't calling upon Julia Child. They make the frigging cookie dough, slice it, put it in the oven, take it out, and put it on a plate. Just how long does that take? And then it occurred to me. I used to tell Vic in New York that if I'm not happy, nobody's happy. If I'm not happy, nobody in this house is happy. And I stopped dead in the middle of the laundromat, and it occurred to me, you know what, that's the reason, that's it right there. It runs backwards. I used to say that if I'm not happy, nobody's happy. That's what it is—they are not happy.

She Has an Influence

So I went to work at the laundromat, got on the phone to Anne, Lieutenant Colonel Coffey's wife, and I said "okay, let me tell you something. Can we say I quit? Can we say I am not doing this any more? Can we say I will never be humiliated like this ever again?" I went on for an hour and a half and told her every frigging thing.

I said, "this is unreal. They are not only working nights, but they're working weekends. Not only are they working weekends, but we are told they are working 9 to 12, and then they work them until 4:20 and tell the married soldiers that they aren't allowed to go home to eat." I said, "you want to know cruel and inhuman?" I said, "Leavenworth feeds their prisoners." I said, "they worked them from 9 to 4:20 with no food. The only food in that motor pool is a damn drinking fountain that tastes like lead poisoning. They just had the pipes fixed in it. My husband left home with a cup of coffee because he was going to work 9 to 12 and be home for lunch." I said, "this is just plain out cruel; this is mean; it's insensitive; and it's irresponsible. I don't know what is going on in this Army, but in every other place in this world, U.S. Army enlisted men are entitled to three meals a day, okay. It is straight up cruel. These guys are coming home angry, pissed, and annoyed, and the only people that they can take it out on is their wives. And you know what? If the soldiers aren't happy, the wives aren't happy, and I can't sit there and say 'hi' like the village idiot. 'I'm Toni the Family Support Group leader. How are you, and could you bake us a cake, thanks, bye-bye.' They don't want to hear it. They're like 'yeah right, fuck you.' And they keep going. If the husbands aren't happy, they aren't going to do shit for me. I look like the village idiot, like I don't know what's going on. I am surprised somebody hasn't asked me what color the sky is in my world." I said, "Anne, I run around saying 'the battalion knows about it, Jim knows about it, the company is handling it, they know what is going on.' I have people coming to my house asking me to write IG complaints, okay?"

So it comes down to an hour and a half on the phone with Anne, and she's like, "all right, Toni what we can do, let's don't get excited, let's not get crazy, this is what we are going to do, just wait. We'll talk to the Chaplain. I'll call Bob. I'll do this." Anything to stop me from quitting FSG. If she could have given me a salary, she would have done it.

"No," I said, "you don't understand. You are not doing this to me anymore. I don't care who you do it to. I can soothe my husband's burns. Every time they burn him, I can cover that, but you are not going to humiliate me like this. You are not going to embarrass me like this. You are not doing it, okay. You are not breaking me from this one time, but you are not doing this to me ever again, okay. Once burned—"

Then she comes up with "we can hang a suggestion box." I said, "Anne, how many times I got to tell you. I've been telling you this since June, they won't put suggestions in the box. It won't happen, because they have been so beat up. Every time they open their mouth, they are beat up. Every time they suggest something to do or something to correct, it's 'shut up you asshole,' or 'shut up you idiot,' or 'you know what? You are working late; you go home; you eat your pork chop sandwich; and you get your butt back here by 1830.' They don't talk any more. They found out it is safer to shut up and do as they do, okay. They are biting the bullet."

At this point I am on the point of whining to Anne and in the back of my head I am thinking I sound like a whiny wife. I am sitting there going "Anne, I can't tell you what the rest of the company has going through their heads, except for the wives that sit in my dining room and tell me that I am going to sit and write IG complaints and sit on the phone with me for two hours telling me, 'Toni I can't believe you do this,' okay. Those are the ones I can tell you about. I am not going to tell you who they are, but I can tell you I have done it." I said, "these are the soldiers that come to me at 10:30 in the morning at work hysterically crying because of what is going on in that motor pool, and I stand there telling these people that the battalion knows about it and they are doing their best. 'Jim is trying to handle it. The company knows about it.' And I look like the village idiot. Well, I am not doing it anymore. I am not going to be your idiot, okay?" I made this call strictly for myself.

This was 11:00. By 1:00 I had the battalion chaplain, a lieutenant colonel, sitting in my laundromat having a cigarette with me. The chaplain has only been back in the United States for four days at this point. Every couple of weeks, this man is deployed somewhere. He just got back from Egypt. He's been home three days. At the end of the month, you get officer reviews—OERs—things like that. Well, even the colonel gets one. This is the status, I found out the lieutenant colonel chaplain, who we just call chaplain, is the one who does what they call climate control. The chaplain has been back three days now at this point. The colonel said to him, "Find out what the hell is going on in [Headquarters Company]. Captain Northway has been there only since July. He got in in July, and it's now September. He's written more Article 15s in the months that he has been there than I did in two and a half years as a company commander. Go find out what the hell is going on over there."[17]

What's happening is that Article 15 is supposed to be the end-all punishment. You get counseling statements, you get extra duty, etc. But you end up on the MP blotter report, and you can be assured that

---

[17]An article 15 is a way of administering punishment for relatively minor infractions; it is "nonjudicial" in that it avoids military court. The defendent must agree to having the issue dealt with under its provisions. The punishment is limited, although a company-grade officer (captain and below) cannot give as much punishment as a field-grade officer (major and above).

you will get an Article 15. Reckless endangerment, evading police, felony misdemeanor stuff, these will get you an Article 15. Northway was passing them out left and right. From what I've gathered since then, is that this is his first command, and Northway was following the advice of his NCOs. His NCOs recommended it, so if NCO Johnson walks in and says "Article 15 for Daniello," or this one walks in and says "Article 15 for Schwartz," he did it.

Northway is not that bad a guy. He let Victor off twice. He really is an innocent, but he is ineffective. I tried to explain to Anne, and to the chaplain, while he was sitting there. I said you know you have ineffective command. Straight up. I am telling you how I see it—ineffective. I said, your motor pool sergeant knows every living, breathing, moving, itching, squealing, looking, blinking thing in that motor pool. He can tell you in any given moment where any given person is and he is as ineffective as I am running that place. Because he doesn't have the support structure. He puts something out to Johnson. Johnson puts it out to them.

For example, it turns out, as I learned from Chaplain Kelly, that junior enlisted soldiers weren't supposed to work that Saturday, and the only ones that did work was Vic's platoon. What the XO[18] had put out, was that it was supposed to be NCOs and up. XO put out, "if it's not done by Friday, NCOs are here Saturday morning." Johnson put out: "if it ain't done by Friday, you are all here for it." Also, the colonel had put out that any time done on a weekend or night, any extra duty, any night work, or any weekend work has to be cleared through him. We in [Headquarters Company] know they are not clearing anything through battalion. The battalion doesn't know anything about this. They don't know they are working weekends. They don't know they are working nights. They don't know they are working past 3:00 on Marne Time Fridays.[19] They don't know they are working after 5:00.

---

[18]Executive officer (second in command).

[19]Ft. Stewart had a policy of ending the work day for most personnel at 3:00 on Fridays, and this was called "Marne Time."

I made $200.16 at that bake sale. Five plates. I had $200.16 in my hands and that was after whatever we purchased. I think we purchased maybe a total of $18 worth of stuff between tape, plastic bags, cookies, and cakes. I made $200.16. Don't nobody ever tell me I can't work magic. So I get home from this bake sale that afternoon. I went down there and relieved the girls and cleaned up and got everything done, brought whatever was left to the company, made some more money at the company. I just wanted to drop it off in the orderly room and go. I didn't want to look at it any more. I was tired of thinking about it. They are so miserable.

At 4:30 I was at company with the bake goods that were left. I was in with the XO. So I was sitting in the XO's office that afternoon of bake sale day, telling her this is how it is, and this is what I did, and I'll tell you straight up I did it, and I will tell you what's wrong. And she just sat there and listened. She was a West Point cadet. She is a West Point graduate. She knows "sucks." If you get through West Point, you know the bottom of the pit. From what I saw, the way they carry themselves, you know they just didn't walk in and learn it. They lived it and ate it. So I am sitting there in the XO's office and the next thing you hear is "Attention!" and everybody's feet go together and I am looking at the XO, and we are behind closed doors so she doesn't have to move. We sit there for a minute and both of us stop talking, then we hear, "At ease!" The XO's office is right next to the captain's office. The only thing separating them is a cinder block wall, and dropped ceilings. We heard the door open, we heard the door close, and it didn't close. It didn't slam, but it didn't close. It was *firmly* closed. The next thing you hear is "tell me what happened on Saturday" coming out Lieutenant Colonel Carson's mouth. Poor Captain Northway has been on Lieutenant Colonel Carson's carpet so many times he's got personal footprints there.

I told the XO, "there have been governments overthrown for less abuse than what these guys have gone through," and she actually sat there and I couldn't believe it came out of her mouth because it was so self-centered for a West Point graduate, for a lieutenant, she sat there and said, "Well, I hope they are not mad at me." And at that point it occurred to me, as I looked at her hair. She has nice hair, dyed

red with highlights. You know, she is still a woman. I sit there looking at her as a lieutenant and I forget she's still a woman.

They pulled Johnson out of motor pool that very minute. Told
her she was restricted from being in the motor pool. Within seven
days, they transferred her. They are investigating her for misuse of
government property, misappropriation, and forgery. She is with a
different unit now. She was also sent with a flag saying she was under
investigation for these things. Don't leave her alone with anything
under E-4.

The night after the bake sale, I called Anne. Anne wasn't home
and I got the lieutenant colonel. He promptly told me, "listen, Anne
and I talked about what you two talked about, and just between me
and you, nobody in this battalion will know that it came from you."

But it was the fastest I ever saw the Army move. Seven days. I
have never seen the Army move so damn fast in my whole life.

HER SUMMARY

The bad things about the Army is trying to adapt to something
other than a 9 to 5 schedule, trying to figure out when should I make
dinner. It's a matter of I can't cook it because I don't know. I can't
plan weekends. There are a lot of nights he's just walked in; and he
gets a call, and he has to go back. What they tend not to do is to tell
you enough ahead of time. They tell you at 4:00 that you are staff
duty driver tonight, which means that he works from 4 that morning,
because they called an alert, 'til 4 that afternoon, told him to go home
to eat, get a razor and shaving cream, and report to battalion for staff
duty driver, and he won't be off until 9 or 10 o'clock next day. That's
a 36 hour day. All right, you will have to do that in the field sometimes, but that's a training field. But then when they get back and they
are supposed to return the truck, and the dude don't show up with
the gas to fill the truck up, and so on, it's frustrating. It's hard to plan.
It bothers me that way. I can adjust if it's not so varied. I get phone
calls at 2 in the morning from sergeants who do not say, "hi, this is
Sergeant Johnson, can I speak to Private Daniello?" I answer the

phone "hello," and a voice barks "Daniello!!" He gets on the phone. I hear them yell, "Daniello, motor pool, BDUs, 0-6." Click.

The good things about being an Army spouse. Personally, I like that he's happy. He loves what he does. I like that he likes what he does. He is learning a trade. I like the fact that he's got passion for what he does. He wants to make it a career, which is surprising, because he wouldn't answer that question in the first year, but now we are into the second year, and we have two years more for the first enlistment, and he's looking to re-up. "The first duty station is their choice, the next one is ours, honey."

CHAPTER 5
Conclusion

These three interviews are a subset of over 100 interviews with
military spouses, as well as additional interviews with military personnel and other individuals in the military community conducted in
the course of dissertation research. Throughout these interviews, a
common stereotype of junior enlisted military spouses emerged,
which was shared not only by more-senior military personnel and
their spouses but also by other junior enlisted soldiers and spouses,
many of whom would discuss their peer group negatively, even when
they shared similar attributes. This stereotype characterizes junior
enlisted spouses as lower class—and thus uneducated and unintelli-
gent, out of control both sexually and reproductively, in unstable
relationships and lacking morals, financially irresponsible, poorly
groomed, inappropriately dressed, and lacking both proper manners
and housekeeping skills. The junior enlisted soldiers and their
spouses were also perceived as childlike in many ways, requiring the
care and attention of the more-mature NCOs and officers, especially
those in leadership positions, such as first sergeant and company
commander. These leaders often spend a large percentage of their
time counseling junior enlisted soldiers to help them resolve their
financial problems, family woes, and other nagging problems.

The three interviews within this book were selected both for their
similarities and dissimilarities to the common stereotype. Of course,
these interviews represent only three cases, although they do reflect
many of the experiences and attitudes portrayed by other military
spouses interviewed during the course of this research. Additionally,
this research focused mainly on two bases, which were deliberately
selected to include military families living in potentially stressful situations. These bases were selected because they were perceived as

being typical of bases with deployable units (as opposed to bases that focus on training and education). The majority of junior enlisted personnel are located at such bases, and almost all Army families spend at least part of their time at such bases. Thus, although the results cannot be generalized across the entire Department of Defense or even the entire Army, the results appear to capture the experiences of a significant number of junior enlisted spouses in light of the larger set of interviews.

The following overviews briefly recap each woman's story.

OVERVIEW OF DANA'S EXPERIENCE

Twenty-year-old Dana lives an isolated life in a trailer park away from the military post and thousands of miles away from her parents and her in-laws. She is not involved with the unit Family Support Group, although she has offered her services when the unit has asked for assistance. She did well in high school, has some college credits, and has some limited intent to return to college but does not necessarily have the means or ambition to complete a college degree. She has two young children, both the result of unintended pregnancies. The children exacerbate extensive financial difficulties, which have come about for several reasons. First, her husband seems to be unaccustomed and unwilling to live within their means. Their initial home selection, new-car purchase, and the acquisition of an expensive set of encyclopedias saddled them with debts that have destroyed their ability to respond to crises. His purchase of a $2,000 car stereo has further endangered their financial well-being. For example, when she needed to replace two tires on her car, she had to do business with a merchant who would extend them credit. This resulted in exorbitantly expensive tires at an extraordinarily high rate of interest—50 percent—to be paid back over a relatively short period, 6 months. Likewise, because they cannot afford to make car payments, they are sinking resources into a title pawn to hold repossession at bay, without reducing the amount owed. Second, they retain some unnecessary expenses, including a cellular phone and rent on the storage space for additional belongings. Third, because they are not living in military quarters, they are not eligible for food stamps. The housing allowance they receive raises their income above qualifying limits. However, after their monthly allotments are deducted from his salary and the bills discussed earlier are paid, they are left with $541. Importantly, this budget does not reduce their debt principal. Further, this amount hinges upon the receipt of separate rations; if he is gone for an entire month, they may have as little as $112 with which to purchase food, diapers, and any other necessities.

OVERVIEW OF JENNIFER'S EXPERIENCE

Jennifer is both similar to and different from the other two. This spouse is extremely young, relatively immature, and has a poor history of family planning. Having married as a pregnant 16-year-old, Jennifer is a 17-year-old mother living far away from her west coast family. Nonetheless, and despite the extreme handicap of being too young to drive in the state of Georgia, she and her husband have managed to overcome the financial traps of the military system. They did so largely thanks to the largesse and guidance of his parents, who have military experience. Jennifer and her husband live in a nice, but modest, two-bedroom condominium, which they purchased with the cosignature of his parents. The mortgage and living expenses are considerably less than most rental properties in town, even without considering any tax benefits or equity gained. She is involved with the unit through the Family Support Group and has made a network of young friends through this association, although she still suffers somewhat from the lack of a peer group (because of her especially young age). This young couple is surviving in the military system largely because of the initial guidance and support of family members, which safeguarded against the typical crippling financial errors.[1]

OVERVIEW OF TONI'S EXPERIENCE

Toni is an older, more mature woman, with a college degree, professional experience, a can-do attitude, and a generosity of spirit that she applies to the entire unit in the capacity of Family Support Group

---

[1]The financial situations of junior enlisted are discussed in greater detail in Margaret Cecchine Harrell, *Brass, Rank and Gold Rings: Class, Race, Gender, and Kinship Within the Army Community*, Dissertation, University of Virginia, Charlottesville, 2000.

leader. At the time of the interview, she served as FSG leader for her husband's company. She has since accepted the role of FSG leader for the entire battalion. Toni does not fit the typical stereotype, except for the financial difficulties. While their living expenses are higher than their living allowance, they are typical of rental costs for the area for a modest home. The only way to lower the expenses (other than receiving military housing) would be to move into a trailer park, which would incur moving expenses and penalties for breaking the lease on their home. When she selected the home, Toni believed she was making a modest selection. At the time of the interview, they drove an older, largely undependable car, which was completely paid for, but which—she felt—both required and justified the cellular phone. Since the interview, they have purchased a modest new car, but she traveled by bus from Georgia to New York to purchase the vehicle at 0.9 percent interest, at the same price that was available from local car dealers at double-digit interest rates. Their only other "extra" expense is cigarettes, which they admit is an unfortunate addiction. However, given the pressures in their lives, they cannot foresee giving up this indulgence.

Perhaps their most significant personal problem results from their inability to conceive a healthy pregnancy. At the time of this writing, she had had her fifth miscarriage, the most recent occurring while her husband was deployed abroad. These unsuccessful pregnancies have deteriorated her emotional and mental health, as well as their financial well-being, because the military medical system would not cover the termination of her prior pregnancy with an extremely sick fetus. To survive financially, Toni works at a job that she finds extremely unappealing because, despite her professional experience, the local job market did not provide alternative opportunities for her. She plans to terminate this employment when they receive military housing, which will reduce their living expenses. However, the recent disciplinary action that reduced her husband by a rank was a double blow: It cut their income and increased the waiting time for military quarters.

Nonetheless, Toni is the main support of many other young enlisted spouses. At the time of this writing, the unit had just returned from its first deployment abroad in many years. Because the unit had previously benefited from a relatively stable and predictable work schedule, many of the soldiers had second jobs to supplement their military incomes. Thus, the deployment struck these families especially hard, and Toni had to deal with multiple, severe emotional and financial crises during the deployment. Of additional importance in this story is that Toni is an individual motivated and capable enough to produce change in a unit that was suffering from severe personnel problems. Despite a positive and competent senior command, there were extreme problems at the lower levels that were not addressed until Toni provided information, through the chain of command of military spouses, to the battalion commander himself. Despite this motivation and ability, she can neither resolve her husband's problems nor affect his success in the unit to the extent that her level of participation might were he an officer and she an officer's wife. She is also unable to live within the financial constraints of the military system.

Stereotypical Women?

These three women might be considered stereotypical junior enlisted spouses. First, while all three of the spouses profess the importance of education, none of them completed college directly after high school. Toni did return to school after an intervening decade, but the other two spouses have not completed their degrees. None of the three "did things in the correct order," in that none of the three attended college and completed her degree prior to their marriage. In fact, Jennifer did not complete her high school equivalency examination until after her marriage and the birth of her son. Thus, all three fulfill the class-based stereotypical lack of education, placed within the expected order of life events.

Two of the three embody the stereotyped characteristic of uncontrolled procreation. Dana was experiencing her second accidental pregnancy, and Jennifer married after she became pregnant. While one of the spouses, Dana, acknowledged having experienced marital problems, the other two relationships appeared relatively solid. However, Toni did acknowledge an overwhelming sense of instability among the lives of the enlisted personnel in her husband's unit when she discussed her difficulty contacting them due to "divorce, disconnects, and no phones. So either they moved, they lost [phone] service, they changed [their phone] number for some reason."

Two of the three couples experience the financial problems perceived to characterize their class. Dana and her husband have severe financial problems that only increase when a crisis occurs, such as having to purchase new tires. While she is trying to manage their financial situation, her husband makes irresponsible purchases, such as a new car stereo. Such behavior puts his desires ahead of family needs. Additionally, the couple also purchased an expensive set of encyclopedias, a questionable decision given the free availability of encyclopedia contents over the Internet. Also, Dana mentions the past financial difficulties of her own parents, suggesting that she is familiar with financial stress. Toni is financially capable, but she and her husband have financial problems because they are not able to support themselves on his military salary without the income from her extremely unpleasant job. Jennifer and her husband are financially stable, if not secure. Their income and expenses balance, largely because of the intervention and assistance of her in-laws.

All three of the couples have either inquired about or currently receive federal assistance. The two mothers both receive WIC benefits, and Dana and Toni have both inquired about food stamps, but both were declared ineligible because of their housing allowances. Jennifer has declined to apply for food stamps. Interestingly, she and Dana both feel differently about WIC benefits than they do about food stamps. They do not perceive WIC to have the negative connotations of "welfare," as food stamps do.

All three of the women work, or have worked, in minimum-wage jobs consistent with their class status, and the two spouses with children both arranged dollar-an-hour daycare for their children. This type of daycare arrangement would be unacceptable to many mothers, given that it is unlicensed, unauthorized by the military community, and unsupervised care by an untrained care-provider. However, this quality of care is all these women can afford.

These women are also relatively isolated from the military base and are not necessarily interested in taking advantage of the military support programs that exist to help them. Even Toni, who dedicates a considerable amount of her time to the Family Support Group system, questions why she does so. Further, all the women speak of the separation between officers' wives and themselves and clearly place themselves within a different social class.

Given these issues, it would not be difficult to characterize these women as being stereotypical and embodying many of the negative features attributed to the junior enlisted community, and many critics will do so. This approach reaffirms the stereotype and excuses many of their problems as being self-inflicted as a result of immaturity, lack of intelligence, or poor decisions. However, this approach also neglects the systemic contributions to their situations and the degree to which these women are struggling to remain within the military community. Indeed, all three of these women are very committed to their marriages and to their husbands' careers; none of these women has left her spouse to return to the familiarity of her family home. Although occasional purchases are well beyond their means, none of these women indulge in regular extravagances. They do not spend their money on expensive meals, partying, or drinking. None of the three have elaborate wardrobes or enjoy extravagant vacations, and all of the women work (or have worked) to contribute to the upkeep of their households. Despite her prior professional experience, Toni works in an unpleasant job because that is all that is available. Dana, who is in the worst financial situation, has tried to compensate for prior poor purchasing decisions with a systematic budgeting approach that has included a negotiation process with local merchants. And Jennifer has even had the foresight and maturity to request a long-distance lock on their phone.

These three women provide a valuable understanding of the military system. Although each partially portrays the negative stereotype of junior enlisted military spouses, understanding their situations provides a deeper understanding of the inadequacy of the stereotype to explain the problems military families face. For example, were their problems explainable primarily by immaturity, sexual irresponsibility, or the lack of education, Jennifer would experience the most desperate problems with military life, which is not the case. While she was compelled to marry young, and lacked even a high school diploma during this research, she and her husband live a balanced—albeit tightly constrained—financial existence, and she enjoys some limited involvement with her husband's unit and other young spouses. Further, were the problems of junior enlisted spouses easily attributable to immaturity, stupidity, an unwillingness to become informed regarding the resources available to them within the military community, or a resistance to becoming a part of the military community, Toni, a mature, educated woman actively involved in the military community, would not experience such difficulty making military life work for her and her husband. Instead, it becomes apparent that, although (in Dana's instance) a few poor initial decisions can continue to plague a young couple without respite, even couples that try to make all the "right" decisions can still struggle financially and emotionally within the constraints of military life.

CONCLUSION

These life-history interviews were conducted to provide a voice to junior enlisted spouses, who tend to be anonymous and unheard within the military community. I selected these three women for extended interviews because they both support and challenge the class-based stereotypes of junior enlisted spouses. While these are the stories of only three women, they capture the experiences of the many other junior enlisted spouses I interviewed during the course of this research, and their problems are consistent with the challenges other junior enlisted Army spouses face.

All of these spouses recognized certain barriers that they face in their everyday lives and that were a constant among many spouses I interviewed. One of these is the separation between officers and junior enlisted personnel, which carries over to the spouses. Dana describes the social barriers between officers and enlisted spouses, and Toni is aware that her friendship with the battalion commander's wife is an exception to the general situation. Many enlisted wives are also isolated from other enlisted spouses, either by their own choice (because they feel many of their peers fit the negative stereotype) or because they live far from the military post and do not have the opportunity to meet other Army enlisted spouses. The military leadership and policymakers should be aware that the experiences of military spouses differ considerably by rank and should strive to consider the views of junior personnel and their families when establishing policies. This work is intended to contribute to an understanding of these families.

Another barrier is the separation between the wife's private life and her husband's professional life. This separation is very different from the experience of officers' spouses, who tend to maintain a more active community among themselves and are often expected to participate in unit activities and/or social gatherings. In contrast, the wives of enlisted soldiers are more likely to be isolated from both unit and post activities and resources. This results, in part, from the conscious decision of many male enlisted soldiers to isolate their wives and to keep them uninformed about unit activities or post resources. Thus, efforts to contact and involve military spouses that are not mailed directly to the spouse at the home address often do not reach them; soldiers cannot be counted on to relay information or invitations.

This isolation is further exacerbated by the small percentage of junior enlisted families residing in military housing. Because many of these families live far from the military base and own only one vehicle, the wives are left home alone without the means to travel to the military base and take advantage of the resources there. Army Community Services' outreach efforts are well-intended but are often grossly undermanned to inform and to encourage the involvement of young spouses, especially spouses who are not native English-speakers. This work indicated the extent to which the lack of military housing is also a contributing factor in the most severe problem of most young enlisted families: financial hardship.

Because these interviews were confined to military families, we cannot make comparisons with similar families in civilian life. Therefore, we cannot say whether financial problems, for example, are more prevalent in civilian families or in military families. More-extensive and more-systematic data would be needed to assess the effects of civilian versus military environments on such problems. Many analysts maintain that enlisted soldiers are paid adequately considering their education and professional experience. However, that position fails to consider key differences between civilian and military employment, and thus the invalidity of any direct comparison of wage rates. First, many Army spouses are unable to contribute to the household income to the same extent they would in a civilian circumstance. This is because Army posts are often located among economically depressed areas, where spouses cannot find adequate employment. Frequent moves also exacerbate this problem by denying spouses the opportunity to develop tenure and experience. Additionally, civilian employers often actively resist hiring military spouses because of the turnover. The irregular schedule of Army soldiers also makes it difficult for spouses to work; they are often unable to depend on their soldiers to watch the children, share the family vehicle, etc. Indeed, while soldiers are deployed, many spouses who have children find it especially difficult to work and care for their families.

Second, the living expenses of many young couples are different while in the Army than they would be at home, where they might live with their parents or depend on a family member to provide child care.

Third, military work schedules prevent most soldiers from obtaining a second job, which would boost their family income were they working in a civilian context. Additionally, unlike many civilian jobs, which pay overtime, the Army expects long hours but does not compensate for additional time worked.

Fourth, the monthly income of many junior enlisted families varies considerably, based upon the deployment schedule of the unit. Should the soldier spend some time either deployed or in the field, some of his separate rations will be deducted. While the Army maintains that this amount is intended only to feed the soldier, the reality for many of these families is different. For these families, a steady and dependable amount would help them avoid crisis. A system that would pay them a predetermined constant amount, based on the unit's planned deployment or training schedule, would grant these families more control over their finances.[2]

Another factor of the financial hardships many junior enlisted military families evidence is extreme debt. Because of the allotment system—whereby merchants, landlords, and others are paid directly by the government from a soldier's wages—soldiers are offered debt opportunities for which they would not qualify were they civilians with the same income. Thus, young soldiers purchase cars, stereos, and other extravagant items beyond their financial means. The allotment system raises the question of the extent to which the military should behave paternalistically, either by limiting the merchants with whom military personnel can do business or by eliminating allotment agreements between merchants and junior enlisted personnel. Unfortunately, while some individuals will argue that the military should not be so involved in personal lives, these issues do negatively affect the military workplace, as company commanders and first sergeants report that large percentages of their time are occupied with the personal financial problems of their soldiers.

The everyday reality depicted here has implications for military leaders and policymakers concerned with the military programs and institutions that serve or affect the junior enlisted community. But because no solution will fit all members of the military community, determining the most appropriate role for the military in addressing problems like those described in this book is difficult. The qualities and experiences of the population vary tremendously. While many of the problems junior enlisted soldiers and their spouses experience are financial and thus related to the pay structure, pay increases are not necessarily the best way to solve the problems. Some other possible changes are mentioned explicitly or are implied herein, such as stabilizing the payment structure for separate rations and eliminating allotment payment agreements between junior enlisted personnel and

---

[2]Soldiers are not supposed to lose their separate rations when deployed overseas, but there have been instances in which deployments labeled "training missions" or other technicalities have precluded families from receiving separate rations while their soldiers are gone.

merchants. Such changes, which could likely be implemented without negative effects on the rest of the military community, deserve consideration but require closer scrutiny. Other changes, however, would impose significant costs and thus are more problematic. For example, any reallocation of military housing to provide greater benefit to junior enlisted personnel would have obvious negative ramifications for the rest of the military community, for which there would be less housing. Evaluating the effects of existing family support programs was beyond the scope of this analysis. Clearly, additional research is needed to determine the best institutional and programmatic solutions for the problems described in this work.

In conclusion, these three stories are intended to provide a window into the experiences and attitudes of junior enlisted spouses. The predicaments of these couples are a combination of systemic constraints, poor financial decisions, and personal crises. To the extent that the problems experienced by Dana were based upon a combination of personal crisis and poor financial decisions, it is important to note that her story was very typical of many heard through the course of this research and that the problems she faced balancing limited and unpredictable income with increasing debt and impulsive acquisitions were characteristic of many junior enlisted couples. Jennifer, the spouse surviving most successfully within the constraints of the system, is also perhaps the least likely candidate to do so: a teenage mother. However, she and her husband benefit from the advantage of family military experience, guidance, and resources unavailable to the other two couples. Toni, who has become actively involved in the military system and has done things the "right" way (by avoiding debt, working, becoming involved in the Family Support Group) is struggling with difficulties. Additionally, although more-senior military personnel and their spouses frequently assert that many of the problems within the junior enlisted community result from young couples having children before being financially able to support them, Toni and her husband are an example of a childless couple that is still having financial difficulties.

The problems these three women have experienced and the trade-offs they have made as part of being Army wives are typical of those of many junior enlisted spouses, regardless of race, age, family situation, or base to which the husband is assigned. These examples demonstrate the common pitfalls of life in the junior enlisted community, the isolation and invisibility of most of these spouses, and how very precarious the lives of these families can be.

Glossary

EO	Equal Opportunity
FSG	Family Support Group—organization at the unit level to assist with family problems, particularly when the unit is deployed
GED	General Equivalency Diploma
ID	Identification—the Armed Forces identity card also carried by certain family members
IG	Inspector General—office to assist soldiers, conduct inquiries into complaints
LES	Leave and Earnings Statement—the military paystub
MGIB, MGI	Montgomery G.I. Bill—tuition assistance
MOS	Military Occupational Specialty—the code for an individual's career area in the Army
MP	Military Police
NCO	Noncommissioned officer
NTC	National Training Center—training site located at Ft. Irvine, California
OSHA	Occupational Safety and Health Administration
PCS	Permanent Change of Station—a move to another Army post
PT	Physical training—Army exercise program
PX	Post Exchange—on-post department store
RDF	Rapid Deployment Force—a force kept at a higher level of readiness
ROTC	Reserve Officer Training Corps—on-campus commissioning program
SAT	Scholastic Aptitude Test
TRICARE	The Department of Defense healthcare program for military families and retirees

UCDPP, DPP	Uniform Clothing Deferred Payment Plan—a credit service for purchases in the Military Clothing Sales Store
WIC	Women, Infants, Children—a program of the Department of Agriculture providing nutrition and education
XO	Executive officer—the officer second in command

MILITARY RANKS AND PAY GRADES

Junior Enlisted

E-1	Private (PV1)
E-2	Private (PV2)
E-3	Private First Class (PFC)
E-4	Corporal or Specialist

Noncommissioned Officers

E-5	Sergeant (SGT)
E-6	Staff Sergeant(SSG)
E-7	Sergeant First Class (SFC)
E-8	Master Sergeant (MSG) or First Sergeant (1SG)
E-9	Sergeant Major (SGM), Command Sergeant Major (CSM) or Sergeant Major of the Army

Officers

O-1	First Lieutenant
O-2	Second Lieutenant
O-3	Captain
O-4	Major
O-5	Lieutenant Colonel
O-6	Colonel

O-7	Brigadier General
O-8	Major General
O-9	Lieutenant General
O-10	General